Interior design by Chelsea Cole. Cover design by Chelsea Cole and Carly Jayne. Photography by Chelsea Cole.

For more information, please contact Chelsea Cole at chelsea@aducksoven.com.

ISBN 978-0-9980499-3-9

SOUS VIDE
MEAL PREP

Chelsea Cole

TABLE OF CONTENTS

HI! I'M CHELSEA

A LITTLE ABOUT ME...

I'm a cookbook author and food blogger born, raised, and still living in Portland, Oregon. I've been blogging at A Duck's Oven for more than 10 years and am passionate about introducing home cooks to the magic of sous vide cooking.

I started sharing recipes through A Duck's Oven in 2010 while a student at the University of Oregon (hence A Duck's Oven – U of O's mascot is the Ducks!). My mission was to help college students get comfortable in the kitchen and rely a little less on boxed mac and cheese and takeout (although you best believe they have their place). My mission remains the same today, but for all home cooks. I share easy recipes to help folks get started in the kitchen as well as sous vide recipes and tips on my website and in my beginner's interactive guide to sous vide cooking, Sous Vide School.

My love of sous vide began way back in 2017 when my mom got me my first immersion circulator for my birthday. I'd seen them around but thought they were too technical and "sciency" for me. I'm so grateful my mom thought this was nonsense and bought me one anyways.

I published my first cookbook, *Everyday Sous Vide*, in 2018. That cookbook is filled with simple meals any home cook can tackle.

For this cookbook, I wanted to share something a little different: the sous vide meal prep method originally developed by my mom that I quickly adopted. It truly eliminates the "What can I possibly serve for dinner?" question because you'll have a freezer full of options.

FOLLOW ME ON INSTAGRAM	CHECK OUT MY BLOG	SOUS VIDE SCHOOL

To use the QR codes throughout the book, open your phone's camera and hold it over the code. You should see a prompt to open the link!

I didn't grow up loving cooking. Though my mom was a good cook, I could have cared less about participating in the kitchen (unless it was to make cheesy scrambled eggs with eggs from our chickens, teenage Chelsea's specialty). When I moved into my first apartment and no longer had food provided by mom or the dorms, I discovered that cooking was a great way to unwind from a long day of school and work. Even now, cooking is still one of my favorite ways to relax at the end of a long day, paired with a good beer and my husband playing DJ.

Speaking of that guy: meet Eric, my high school sweetheart turned husband and resident taste tester. Though I prefer to be the only cook in the kitchen, he keeps me entertained and my wine glass full.

In my free time, you'll find me at a Timbers soccer game, in a local taproom or restaurant, camping across Oregon, thinking up new ways to prepare the fish and game Eric, my brother, and dad bring home, or spending time with my family on Sauvie Island in Portland.

HOW TO USE THIS BOOK

If you really put this cookbook to work (and I hope you do!), you'll find your freezer stocked with meals that are ready to hit the water bath and be served for dinner. Each day, when someone (maybe even you?) inevitably asks, "What's for dinner?" you'll be able to look in the freezer and provide an answer! It's life-changing.

So, here's what I want you to do:

STEP 1: Go clean out your freezer. Yep, I mean it! It's a pain in the butt, but you don't want to put in all this meal prep work only to find there's nowhere to store your goodies.

STEP 2: Create a system that will allow you to keep track of what's in your freezer. This could be a white board on the freezer door, a note on your phone, or good ol' pen and paper. As long as it's something you'll use and update consistently, it'll work.

STEP 3: Hit your favorite meat supplier, see what's on sale, buy that in bulk, then take it home and prep using whatever recipes catch your eye in this cookbook.

STEP 4: Don't skip the sides! In this cookbook you'll find recipes for green beans, carrots, asparagus, grains, and more that you can have ready and waiting in your freezer. I'm going to be real with you: I'm also a huge proponent of stocking up on things like frozen tater tots, sweet potato fries, and ravioli so you're always able to create a meal.

STEP 5: Throw your meals in the freezer, make note of what you prepped in your system, and rest easy knowing you have several dinners (and maybe some lunches!) taken care of for future you.

STEP 6: Don't forget breakfast! At the beginning of each week, prep egg bites or oatmeal pudding so you have something to just grab from the fridge and heat on busy mornings. My favorite? Low fat, high protein egg bites with goat cheese and turkey bacon.

"But Chelsea, I'm not home all day and can't get something in the water bath hours before dinner time. Help!"

I've got you. Here are some of my favorite ways to work around this:

SOLUTION 1: If your immersion circulator is fancy and has wifi connectivity and an app, you can put your food in an ice bath in your sous vide container before you head to work in the morning. Then start your circulator remotely! Make sure to add an extra 30 minutes of cook time if you do this to allow the water to come to temp. Additional tip: Set an alarm on your phone so you don't forget.

SOLUTION 2: When you start dinner, sous vide tomorrow night's dinner, too. Stick it in the fridge when it's done, then set it on the counter when you get home from work the next day to bring the temperature up. Just follow finishing instructions and serve!

SOLUTION 3: During your usual meal prep time, sous vide several dinner options for the week and then refrigerate. Remove it to the counter when you get home from work to raise the temperature, then follow finishing instructions and serve.

In addition to some very easy to prepare recipes, you'll find some that require a few extra steps or have larger portions for those moments when someone "pops by" for dinner, or you just want to create a meal that's a little *extra*. My personal favorite might be the 48 Hour "Braised" Short Ribs (page 111), but honestly, they're all fantastic. The best part? They're all freezer friendly, so you split the work between whenever you buy and whenever you serve!

But before we get there, let's make sure we all understand the science of sous vide and learn a few techniques to make the whole process a little easier. Read on!

WHAT IS SOUS VIDE?

HOW TO PRONOUNCE SOUS VIDE

No shame in not being totally sure how to pronounce this French cooking term.

Soo (like "moo") veed. Don't pronounce the second "s" and the "i" is a long sound. There ya go!

Curious what that means? Sous vide is a French method of cooking and translates to "under vacuum." People have experimented with different elements of the sous vide cooking process for centuries (low-and-slow cooking, cooking under pressure, etc.) but it was all put together in the 1970s in France.

WHAT DOES IT MEAN TO COOK SOUS VIDE?

To cook sous vide, you put your food in a container (typically a jar or food-safe plastic bag), remove the air, then place it in a water bath at a specific temperature for an extended period of time. So you're providing a consistent temperature throughout the entire cooking environment, usually for slightly longer than you'd normally cook your food.

THINK OF A SOUS VIDE WATER BATH LIKE A MINI HOT TUB

To sous vide, all you have to do is fill a container with water and place an immersion circulator in the water. Like you would set the temperature on a hot tub, you do the same on the immersion circulator.

Once you press "Start", the immersion circulator moves water through its heat coils then back into the water bath. It brings all the water up to your desired temperature and keeps it there for as long as you'd like.

WHY IS THE SOUS VIDE METHOD BETTER THAN OTHER COOKING METHODS?

Buckle up and put on your science hats, friends.

Let's use steak as our example. The temperature of the center of the steak determines its doneness. This means the center of a rare steak is literally colder than the center of a well-done steak.

What is doneness? You know when you're at a restaurant and the server asks "How do you want this cooked?" and you say "Medium-rare, please" (or at least I hope you do)? That's doneness.

Using an immersion circulator, you can keep a water bath at a precise temperature. I like a medium-rare strip steak, and to achieve that, the internal temperature of the steak should be 129 degrees F. When I place a vacuum-sealed steak in a water bath set to this temperature, it never has the opportunity to cook any hotter than 129 degrees F because the entire cooking environment is 129 degrees F.

Let's say you cook the steak in your oven at 425 degrees F. You have to pull your steak out at that magical, unknown moment the center reaches 129 degrees F or you'll overcook it. That's a big ask! Especially because ovens (and grills and stoves) tend to have "hot spots" where some parts get hotter than others. Not so with a temperature controlled water bath!

In a sous vide water bath, I could cook that steak for days and it would still be rare because it's all about temperature. You're reading this correctly: you'll never ruin a good cut of meat again. You can't overcook it, no matter how long you cook it. (You can make the texture weird by cooking it too long, but we'll talk about that in a bit.)

OTHER BENEFITS OF SOUS VIDE COOKING

In addition to the obvious, sous vide cooking is wonderful because you can get a tougher cut of meat and cook it long enough to tenderize it while still keeping it rare. The amount of time under heat changes texture.

For the squeamish people out there, you can pasteurize a medium steak, killing all the germs while keeping that lovely texture. No more well-done steaks for our germaphobes! To learn more about sous vide and pasteurization, check out this article by *Cook's Illustrated* on the safety of sous vide.

"IS SOUS VIDE SAFE?"
- COOK'S ILLUSTRATED

Cooking for a crowd? You can prep several servings at once, get the center of the plate prepped hours in advance, then just sear and serve. The Piri Piri Inspired Chicken on page 121 is a perfect example of this!

Yes, you will make a killer steak, amazing pork chops, and top-notch salmon with sous vide. But what else? Make the silkiest egg bites (page 25), perfect asparagus (page 133), and the best fried chicken you've ever had (page 115).

CHELSEA'S SOUS VIDE TERMS

Listen: we're going to play fast and loose with grammar in this book. Sous vide is a noun and a verb here. I will say "sous viding" and "sous vided." Are these technically correct? No. Am I going to do it anyway? Yep.

UNDERSTANDING TIME & TEMP

I want you to repeat this mantra while we dive into understanding time and temp: I will not overthink this. Because it's really easy to get in the weeds with this part.

The basic formula of any sous vide recipe is the amount of time you cook the food and the temperature of your water bath. This is commonly referred to as "time and temp." In shorthand, it looks something like "165F/36 hours."

The beautiful thing about sous vide cooking is that you can't overcook your food.

But the thing is, you kind of can.

The texture of food changes the longer it's exposed to heat hot enough to cook it. So, while you may not be actually changing the "doneness" of your food, you can change the texture. And this - changing texture without changing doneness - is a truly magical thing.

When considering the time and temperature you want to cook at, here are the questions you should ask:

HOW BIG IS THE THING YOU'RE COOKING?
- A lot of people say, "1 hour per inch of thickness," which isn't correct. It's really the bigger the item, the longer the cook time.
- Nearly any "single-serving protein" (i.e. steak, pork chop, chicken breast, etc.) should cook for at least 1 hour, up to 4 hours.
- We often cook big cuts of meat for 6-48 hours depending on what our goals are.

WHAT DONENESS DO YOU WANT?
- When cooking beef and pork, you may want them cooked rare to medium, whereas you'll want chicken cooked differently.

WHAT TEXTURE DO YOU WANT?
- When I cook a pork chop, I want it to be meaty. However, when I cook a pork shoulder, I want it to be fall-apart tender.

WHAT IS YOUR TIMELINE?

○ We do have a few safety rules to consider, one of which is that anything cooked lower than 130 degrees F should not be cooked longer than 3 hours. At this point, harmful bacteria can develop. I am not a food scientist, so I'm going to point you to the *Cook's Illustrated* article linked on the previous page to read more about food temperature safety. If you want to cook longer than 3 hours, cook at 130 degrees F or higher.

HOW DELICATE IS THIS FOOD?

○ You'll see in the protein overviews that seafood requires a much shorter cook time and lower temperatures than other proteins. There's less wiggle room with these cooks.

To help you see what these differences look like, I cooked a few steaks at the same temperature for different amounts of time. The differences are subtle, but they're there. Notice that the texture of meat starts to look more "crumbly" the longer it's cooked.

6 HOURS

4 HOURS

2 HOURS

As you start to sous vide all the things, time and temperature will become more intuitive. Don't sweat it too much for now. Reference the protein overviews and experiment with different times and temperatures to figure out what you like best!

WHAT YOU NEED TO VIDE

There's only one thing you need for sous vide cooking that may not be in your kitchen already: a sous vide machine. That's it. But there are lots of other things that are nice to have, even when you're just starting out.

SOUS VIDE MACHINES

There are three types of sous vide machines:

○ Immersion circulators
○ Water ovens
○ All-in-one machines

Immersion circulators are what I've always used and likely will use forever. They're easy to store, affordable, lightweight, and compact enough to travel with (yep, I'm that person).

I have used several brands of immersion circulators. I recommend going with a well-known and well-reviewed brand. Shop for this gadget like you would any other small appliance: Do some research, ask around, and find out what folks like!

GET MY UP-TO-DATE LINKED LIST OF SOUS VIDE PRODUCTS I RECOMMEND EMAILED TO YOU

Water ovens were the first type of sous vide machine available. They're a container and a circulato in one. Fun fact: Some water ovens can be built into your cabinetry these days!

Personally, I would not get a water oven. They're big, heavy, and difficult to store. They also tend to be a much more expensive option.

All-in-one machines are the newest type of sous vide machine. I'm referring to an Instant Pot-style pressure cooker, sous vide, slow cooker, rice cooker extraordinaire. These machines might seem convenient but they don't truly circulate the water and heat it from the outside in. The temperature of the water won't be as consistent through the bath or as reliable, defeating the purpose of "precision cooking" with sous vide.

FOOD PACKAGING

When it comes to what you cook your food in, there are a few different options for different types of food.

Bags

Here's the deal: I have tried reusable vacuum bags, and they tend to fail after 3-5 uses. Zipper-top freezer bags have their time and place, especially when it comes to liquid heavy recipes, but what I use most are vacuum-sealed bags with my vacuum sealer. Nothing works as well as a vacuum sealer does!

Note: I have heard good things about cooking in large silicone zipper-top bags, but haven't tried it myself. It'll still be a bit of a pain to remove the air.

Jars

When cooking from this cookbook, you'll only need jars for the breakfast items. However, there are so many fun things you can sous vide that you'll need jars for! Check out my first book, *Everyday Sous Vide*, and my blog, A Duck's Oven for lots of fun recipes with jars.

CHECK OUT MY 1ST COOKBOOK, EVERYDAY SOUS VIDE

With jars, you can make:

- Desserts (think cheesecake, creme brulee, flourless chocolate cake!)
- Liquor infusions
- Infused oils
- Pickles
- ... and more!

You can absolutely use standard canning jars. However, my favorite jars are Weck jars. They're more expensive than canning jars so I only have them in the size I need for egg bites (the jarred item I make most frequently).

I love Weck jars because the only metal pieces are the clamps, so there's less rusting. I'm sure if I was more diligent about drying the lids, rusting wouldn't be as big of an issue with my canning jars, but alas, I ... won't do that.

WATER BATH CONTAINERS

When you first start out, you can totally use a stockpot. All you need is a large container that can stand up to 185 degrees F.

Eventually, you may want to get something a little bigger that you can dedicate to sous vide cooking without occupying a beloved stockpot. The containers I use are also clear which allows me to keep an eye on things—especially useful during long cooks!

You can use a Cambro container which can be found at restaurant supply stores like Cash and Carry. I have two bigger ones that I use when cooking large roasts or, say, 30 individual cheesecakes at once (sous vide cheesecake is my go-to treat when I have a booth at events and markets).

OTHER SOUS VIDE ACCESSORIES I LOVE

- A cast iron skillet
- Silicone oven gloves (for pulling hot jars and bags out of hot water)
- A cast iron grill press (they help you get a great sear)
- Silicone-coated magnets or sous vide magnets (for keeping food submerged in water)

AIR REMOVAL METHODS

In order to sous vide successfully, you want to make sure to remove as much air as possible from the bags you're cooking in before they go into the water bath. This prevents them from floating while the food cooks. If the bags float, the food won't cook evenly and could be exposed to bacteria since it's not completely surrounded by temperature-controlled water.

WATCH DEMO VIDEOS FOR AIR REMOVAL METHODS

THE ARM METHOD

This is probably the simplest method in the proverbial sous vide book.

Put your food into a freezer-grade zipper-top bag and squish it all to the bottom. Lay it flat on the counter OR leave just the part with the food hanging off the edge of the counter (helpful if liquid heavy) and zip the bag almost all the way closed.

Place one arm above the food, as close to the food as you can, then take your other arm and slide it from arm to the top of the bag to push the air out, then finish sealing the zipper. It's shockingly effective!

THE WATER DISPLACEMENT METHOD

This method is similar to the "arm" method and works well. This method is great for anything that could be damaged by more aggressive air removal methods like vacuum sealing (for example, the Pimento Cheese Stuffed Burgers on page 113).

Put your food in a freezer-grade zipper-top bag. Fill a large container with water. Pro tip: just use your sous vide water bath before you start heating it.

Zip the bag almost all the way closed. Making sure to keep the zipper out of the water, press the bottom of the bag into the water directing the air towards the opening.

Submerge until just the zipper is above the water, then zip the rest of the way closed.

REUSABLE VACUUM SEAL BAG

Reusable vacuum seal bags are a great sous vide air-removal option because they're designed for sous vide, easy to use, affordable, and a "greener" option.

They have two cons. One, they're a pain in the butt to clean. I turn them inside out, rinse, dish wash or hand wash, then turn right side out and let air dry. Two, they typically quit working after 3-5 uses.

Place the food in the bag then seal the zipper completely. Use the little hand pump that comes with the bag to suck out all the air. Easy, peezy.

VACUUM SEAL

This method is certainly the easiest and the most reliable. Vacuum sealers have a reputation for being expensive, but they don't have to be! You can now find great vacuum sealers for around $70.

Some of my favorite things about using a vacuum sealer: You will never question the seal, your food will easily sink, you don't have to worry about keeping the seal above water, and you don't have to wash anything after. It's just easy.

When buying a vacuum sealer, make sure to purchase one with a manual setting. This allows you to control the amount of air you remove from the bag and seal it at that precise point. This is helpful for delicate foods like meatballs, stuffed burgers, seafood and more that can get "squished," and foods with a small amount of liquid.

CHAMBER VACUUM SEALING

Chamber vacuum sealing requires a chamber vacuum sealer, which comes with some major pros and cons. Let's cover those, starting with the cons:

- They tend to be really big. I have one that I love that lives on my counter and folks mistake it for a small mini fridge.
- They're also really heavy!
- They're expensive. On the inexpensive end, you can find them around $350, but they often cost as much as $1200.

However, they've got some great pros:

- You can vacuum seal liquids! This is the primary pro, especially when it comes to a lot of the recipes in this book. I once vacuum sealed a bag of water to test the limits of my chamber vac and it worked perfectly.
- You can adjust the suction so you can easily vacuum seal delicate items.

Considering the investment of both money and storage space, I would make sure you plan to use a gadget like this a lot before going for it. I use mine all the time so it's more than worth it, but that won't be the case for everyone!

GET MY UP-TO-DATE
LINKED LIST OF SOUS
VIDE PRODUCTS I
RECOMMEND EMAILED
TO YOU

BREAKFAST
BREAKFAST
BREAKFAST
BREAKFAST
BREAKFAST
BREAKFAST
BREAKFAST
BREAKFAST

CLASSIC
EGG BITES

I argue that Starbucks' Sous Vide Egg Bites are what's really helped to popularize sous vide cooking over the last few years, and for good reason! There's nothing like a silky smooth, flavor packed egg bite. But here's the thing: you can make them better and for way less money yourself. One thing I love to do is play with the dairy - try swapping half or all of the heavy cream for other dairies like sour cream, cream cheese, and more!

YOU'LL NEED:

EGG BITE BASE:
6 large eggs
1 cup heavy cream
1 ½ tsp salt
1 tsp ground black pepper

ADDITION IDEAS (QUANTITIES ARE PER JAR):
2 tbsp shredded cheddar + 1 piece cooked crumbled bacon
1 oz gruyere + 2 tbsp cooked diced pancetta
1 oz smoked salmon + 2 tbsp crumbled goat cheese
1 oz feta cheese + 2 tbsp chopped oil packed sun dried tomatoes

1. Preheat a water bath using an immersion circulator to 185 degrees F.

2. Whisk together the eggs and the heavy cream in a large bowl.

3. Pour the egg mixture into 6 half pint jars, dividing evenly between the jars. Add about ¼ tsp salt and a pinch of black pepper to each jar. Evenly distribute your desired additions between the jars.

4. Place undamaged lids on your jars. Close to "finger tight" (you should be able to easily unscrew with just your fingertips). Place jars carefully into water bath (I recommend wearing silicone oven gloves or using a jar lifter for canning). Jars should be completely submerged and you should see small air bubbles escaping the jars. If the jars are floating, your lids are on too tight.

5. Let cook for 30 minutes. Remove from water bath and place on a towel. Let cool slightly before serving, or transfer to fridge once completely cooled.

LOW FAT, HIGH PROTEIN
EGG BITES

While the Classic Egg Bites are amazing, they can be a little heavy. I try to prioritize protein in my diet, so I developed this recipe for low fat, high protein egg bites to enjoy most mornings while saving Classic Egg Bites for special occasions. This version is made a little lighter by swapping some of the eggs for egg whites and the dairy for low fat cottage cheese. These little protein bombs pack a ton of flavor and will leave you feeling fueled for your day!

YOU'LL NEED:

EGG BITE BASE:
2 large eggs
1 cup egg whites (about 8 egg whites)
1 cup low fat, small curd cottage cheese
1 ½ tsp salt
1 tsp ground black pepper

ADDITION IDEAS (QUANTITIES ARE PER JAR):
1 piece crumbled cooked turkey bacon + 2 tbsp of goat cheese
¼ tsp za'atar + 2 tbsp feta cheese
1 tsp pesto + 1 tbsp sun dried tomatoes

1. Preheat a water bath using an immersion circulator to 185 degrees F.

2. Whisk together the eggs, egg whites, and cottage cheese in a large bowl.

3. Pour the egg mixture into 6 half pint jars, dividing evenly between the jars. Add about ¼ tsp salt and a pinch of black pepper to each jar. Evenly distribute your desired additions between the jars.

4. Place undamaged lids on your jars. Close to "finger tight" (you should be able to easily unscrew with just your fingertips). Place jars carefully into water bath (I recommend wearing silicone oven gloves or using a jar lifter for canning). Jars should be completely submerged and you should see small air bubbles escaping the jars. If the jars are floating, your lids are on too tight.

5. Let cook for 30 minutes. Remove from water bath and place on a towel. Let cool slightly before serving, or transfer to fridge once completely cooled.

OATMEAL PUDDING

I'm gonna be up front: this recipe is a little weird. I almost didn't include it because it's so different from traditional baked oatmeal. As Carly, an incredibly helpful recipe tester, pointed out, it's almost a cross between a baked oatmeal and a bread pudding. And so the title became Oatmeal Pudding! For my friends who love a smooth texture, this breakfast is going to be right up your alley.

YOU'LL NEED:

BASE:
1 ¼ cups milk (any milk is fine)
1 cup old-fashioned oats
½ cup light brown sugar, packed
2 large eggs
1 tsp ground cinnamon
½ tsp vanilla extract
½ tsp kosher salt

ADDITION IDEAS (QUANTITIES ARE PER JAR):
2 tbsp berries
¼ banana, sliced + 1 tbsp peanut butter
1 tbsp nutella (Note: add the nutella "ball" without stirring for a delicious, chocolatey center!)
1 tbsp pumpkin puree + ½ tsp pumpkin pie spice
1 tbsp brown sugar + 1 tbsp toasted chopped pecans

1. Preheat a water bath using an immersion circulator to 180 degrees F.

2. Add all base ingredients to a blender and blend until smooth.

3. Pour the mixture into 5 half-pint jars, dividing evenly between the jars. Add your desired additions to the jars and stir.

4. Place undamaged lids on your jars. Close to "finger tight" (you should be able to easily unscrew with just your fingertips). Place jars carefully into the water bath (I recommend wearing silicone oven gloves or using a canning jar lifter). Jars should be completely submerged and you should see small air bubbles escaping the jars. If the jars are floating, your lids are on too tight.

5. Let cook for 1 hour. Remove from water bath and place on a towel. Let cool slightly before serving, or transfer to fridge once completely cooled.

MIX & MATCH

HOW TO USE THIS SECTION

First up, you'll find a comprehensive overview of over a dozen meats and seafoods. These overviews include:
○ Prep instructions, if applicable.
○ Time and temperature options, including my preferred times and temps.
○ Finishing options and instructions, if applicable.

I hope these overviews come in handy beyond this cookbook (although you should definitely try all the recipes in this cookbook!).

Next are plenty of recipes for rubs and marinades to season your meat before freezing, as well as compound butters, salsas, and sauces you can use to finish your meals after you sous vide them.

These recipes are written to work with 1-1.5 pounds of meat. You can absolutely adjust the quantities as needed for what you've got!

All of the meats and seafoods can be mixed and matched with various rubs, marinades, and toppers. See my pairing recommendations by either looking at the protein overview page (helpful if you buy a ton of one type of meat in bulk) or the recipe page.

First, I suggest making all of the Compound Butters (page 106) that catch your eye. They can be frozen for up to 6 months and are great to have on hand if you want to finish a dish with little effort. The same goes for the Rubs (page 54): Make a batch of each now so they're at the ready to season your food.

I pretty much always have a batch of Ashley's Ranch (page 98) ready in the fridge. It's an easy way to add flavor to almost anything, it's especially handy for lunches, and there are some really fun variations (can you say Kimchi Ranch?).

CHICKEN

CHICKEN BREASTS

Seasoned boneless, skinless chicken breasts I can just throw in the water bath are my cheat code for always having healthy lunches ready to go around our house. They're so easy, pack a ton of flavor, and don't require finishing.

My personal favorite time and temp? 150 degrees F for 2 hours (2.5 hours from frozen).

PAIR THEM WITH:

RESULT	TEMP	TIME	TIME (FROZEN)
Very soft texture, little moisture loss	140 degrees F 60 degrees C	2 - 4 hours	3 - 4 hours
Tender and close to "traditional" texture, still juicy	150 degrees F 65 degrees C	1 - 4 hours	2 - 4 hours
Traditional texture, slightly stringy, more moisture loss	160 degrees F 71 degrees C	1 - 4 hours	2 - 4 hours

TO FINISH:

For most of the chicken breast recipes in this cookbook and in general, searing is optional unless explicitly stated otherwise. Although it does look more appetizing, I almost never sear my chicken breasts after sous viding.

If you do want to sear, I recommend a pan sear. Heat a skillet over medium-high heat. Once hot, add butter or oil. Sear until browned, about 1 minute on each side.

CHICKEN TH!GHS

Sous viding has become one of my favorite ways to prepare chicken thighs. I prefer bone in, skin on because they have so much flavor. The times and temperatures below apply to both boneless and bone-in (except the last row).

I love chicken thighs that are just starting to pull away from the bone but still juicy: 165 degrees F for 6 hours.

PAIR THEM WITH:

RESULT	TEMP	TIME	TIME (FROZEN)
Very juicy and firm	150 degrees F 65 degrees C	1 - 4 hours	2 - 4 hours
Juicy, mostly tender	155 degrees F 68 degrees C	1 - 4 hours	2 - 4 hours
Juicy and completely tender	165 degrees F 74 degrees C	1 - 4 hours	2 - 4 hours
Fall off the bone texture (bone-in only)	165 degrees F 74 degrees C	4 - 8 hours	4 - 8 hours

TO FINISH:

FOR BONELESS: Searing is optional. Depending on the dish, you can dice the chicken into large cubes and sear or sear whole. To sear, heat a large skillet over medium-high heat. Once hot, add butter or oil. Add the chicken and sear until browned, about 1 minute on each side.

FOR BONE-IN: Always sear before topping with a sauce. To sear, heat a skillet over high heat until smoking. Add butter or oil and sear skin side down until golden brown, 1-2 minutes. Sear for 1 minute on the other side.

WHOLE CHICKEN

Since the first time I sous vided a whole chicken, I won't cook them any other way. Sous vide guarantees the chicken will be cooked all the way through in every part and oh so juicy!

Always spatchcock your chickens before seasoning and vacuum sealing. Scan this code to see how that's done.

CHICKEN SIZE	TEMP	TIME	TIME (FROZEN)
Small Chicken	155 degrees F 68 degrees C	4 - 5 hours	5 - 6 hours
Medium Chicken (Average grocery store chicken)	155 degrees F 68 degrees C	6 - 7 hours	6 - 7 hours
Large Chicken	155 degrees F 68 degrees C	8 hours	8 hours

TO FINISH:

Always crisp the skin before serving and topping with a sauce. This can be done by searing or broiling.

PAN SEAR: Preheat a large skillet over high heat until smoking. Add butter or oil and sear on both sides until golden brown, about 2-3 minutes.

BROIL: Line a rimmed baking sheet with foil. Preheat your oven's broiler to high. Add chicken to the lined baking sheet, skin side up, and broil until skin is golden and crisped, about 5 minutes depending on your broiler.

CHICKEN OR TURKEY MEATBALLS

Although sous vide may seem "overkill" for meatballs, there's nothing better than remembering you have a batch in the freezer you can throw right in the water bath. Sous vide meatballs are perfectly tender and fully cooked: no risk of dry meatballs!

YOU'LL NEED:

1 lb ground turkey or chicken
1 large egg
½ cup panko bread crumbs
1 tsp onion powder
1 tsp garlic powder
1 tsp Italian seasoning
1 tsp kosher salt
½ tsp black pepper

1. Add all ingredients to a large bowl. Wash your hands and use them to mix everything together.

2. Form into 12 equal sized balls (I like to use an ice cream scoop!). Carefully add all the meatballs to a bag of your choice in a single layer without touching. Gently remove the air (if using a vacuum sealer, use the manual setting and stop the seal as soon as the air is gone).

3. At this point, you can freeze the meatballs or cook immediately.

RESULT	TEMP	TIME	TIME (FROZEN)
Very soft texture, little moisture loss	145 degrees F 63 degrees C	1 - 4 hours	2 - 4 hours
Tender and close to "traditional" texture, still juicy	150 degrees F 65 degrees C	1 - 4 hours	2 - 4 hours
Traditional texture, veering towards dry	160 degrees F 71 degrees C	1 - 4 hours	2 - 4 hours

TO FINISH:

Searing the meatballs is optional, but I think it's worth doing! To sear, heat a large skillet over medium-high heat. Once hot, add about 1 tbsp extra virgin olive oil. Add the meatballs, searing in batches so you don't overcrowd the skillet. Sear on all sides until browned.

PAIR THEM WITH:

Q: WHY CAN I COOK CHICKEN AT A LOWER TEMP THAN 165° F WHEN SOUS VIDING?

A: The information provided by experts like the USDA around food safety often sacrifices detail in favor of being easy to understand. 165 degrees F isn't the full story.

Temperature guidelines are there to make sure you kill bacteria, the big one being salmonella when we're cooking chicken. We want to pasteurize the chicken. Pasteurization is related to both time AND temperature.

The reason 165 degrees F is the gold standard is because chicken is instantly pasteurized at that temperature. The lowest temperature I offer for cooking chicken in this book is 140 degrees F. If your chicken is 140 degrees F all the way through for at least 27.5 minutes, it will be pasteurized! And I recommend a minimum of 2 hours to allow for plenty of time for it to get to temperature and be there for far longer than 27.5 minutes.

At 145 degrees F you only need 9.2 minutes, at 150 degrees F you only need 2.8 minutes, and at 155 degrees F you only need 47.7 seconds! Pretty neat, huh?

TO LEARN MORE ABOUT THIS, CHECK OUT THIS ARTICLE FROM SERIOUS EATS

SEAFOOD

SALMON

Salmon is one of my all time favorite foods. Living in the Pacific Northwest surrounded by fishermen means I'm lucky to have a lot of it!

I was thrilled to discover that, like most other proteins, it can be cooked so perfectly with the magic of sous vide. I like my salmon rare but flaky and stick to 121 degrees F for 30 minutes (45 minutes from frozen).

PAIR IT WITH:

RESULT	TEMP	TIME	TIME (FROZEN)
Very soft, barely cooked	110 degrees F 43 degrees C	30 mins - 1 hour	45 mins - 1 hour
Just starting to flake but still translucent	115 degrees F 46 degrees C	30 mins - 1 hour	45 mins - 1 hour
Very moist and just flaky	120 degrees F 49 degrees C	30 mins - 1 hour	45 mins - 1 hour
Firm and flaky	130 degrees F 54 degrees C	30 mins - 1 hour	45 mins - 1 hour

TO FINISH:

Finishing is optional but can make the salmon better. Here are my two go-to ways:

SKILLET: Heat a skillet over medium-high heat. Once hot, add 1 tbsp of salted butter or extra virgin olive oil. If you like to eat the skin, sear skin side down first until crispy, then flip and sear the meat side. Test it with a spatula every 30 seconds to see if the salmon easily lifts up. Flip or remove to a plate the moment it does.

BROIL: Preheat your oven's broiler to high. Line a rimmed baking sheet with foil. Some sauces, like any of the ranches, are tasty to coat the salmon with before broiling. Otherwise, coat with a thin layer of extra virgin olive oil or melted salted butter. Broil under high heat for 2-3 minutes, until just starting to brown.

WHITE FISH

"White fish" is an umbrella term for any flaky white fish, including cod, halibut, rockfish, bass, and more. I most commonly sous vide cod and halibut.

I like my white fish to be completely flaky while still moist, so I cook at 130 degrees F for 30 minutes (45 minutes from frozen).

PAIR IT WITH:

RESULT	TEMP	TIME	TIME (FROZEN)
Extremely rare, just starting to flake	120 degrees F 49 degrees C	30 mins - 1 hour	45 mins - 1 hour
Moist and flaky	130 degrees F 54 degrees C	30 mins - 1 hour	45 mins - 1 hour
Firm and flaky	140 degrees F 60 degrees C	30 mins - 1 hour	45 mins - 1 hour

TO FINISH:

Finishing is optional but can make the white fish better.

Heat a skillet over medium-high heat. Once hot, add 1 tbsp of salted butter or extra virgin olive oil. Sear each side. Watch it carefully: don't sear too long or you'll overcook it, but if you don't sear long enough, the meat won't easily pull away from the skillet and it might stick. Test it with a spatula every 30 seconds to see if the fish easily lifts up. Flip or remove to a plate the moment it does.

SHRIMP

I mean it when I say that I will not cook shrimp any way but sous vide anymore. Like everything else, sous vide eliminates the risk of over- or under-cooking but also creates the best shrimp texture I've ever had.

I really like a bite on my shrimp while keeping it tender, so I cook mine at 135 degrees F for 30 minutes (45 minutes from frozen).

PAIR THEM WITH:

GOCHUJANG COCONUT MILK MARINADE	PG 59
FAJITA MARINADE	PG 61
BLACK PEPPER ROSEMARY MARINADE	PG 63
THAI INSPIRED BASIL MARINADE	PG 65
THE EVERYTHING MARINADE	PG 67
CLASSIC LEMONY MARINADE	PG 69
CHIPOTLE MUSTARD MARINADE & SAUCE	PG 71
MISO MARINADE	PG 73
CITRUS MARINADE	PG 75
GARLIC BUTTER SAUCE	PG 79
FIRECRACKER PINEAPPLE SAUCE	PG 81
ORANGE HARISSA HONEY GLAZE	PG 83
SWEET ONION BACON SAUCE	PG 91
FIERY PEANUT SAUCE	PG 93
PESTO & SUN DRIED TOMATO SAUCE	PG 97
MANGO SALSA	PG 101
COTIJA CORN SALSA	PG 103
BALSAMIC STRAWBERRY SALSA	PG 105

RESULT	TEMP	TIME	TIME (FROZEN)
Almost raw, good for ceviche	125 degrees F 52 degrees C	15 mins - 1 hour	30 mins - 1 hour
Just starting to firm, tender	130 degrees F 54 degrees C	15 mins - 1 hour	30 mins - 1 hour
Opaque and tender	135 degrees F 57 degrees C	15 mins - 1 hour	30 mins - 1 hour
Tender with snappy bite	140 degrees F 60 degrees C	15 mins - 1 hour	30 mins - 1 hour

TO FINISH:

I don't recommend finishing shrimp - it's perfect right out of the bag and you don't want to risk overcooking it!

SCALLOPS

I love scallops. They're meaty, a little sweet, and take on flavor oh so well. Although brown butter and lemon is a delicious classic, there are so many ways to prepare scallops and I encourage you to use this book to branch out!

My favorite time and temp: 122 degrees F for 30 minutes. I like to go rare for wiggle room for the sear.

RESULT	TEMP	TIME	TIME (FROZEN)
Extremely tender	120 degrees F 49 degrees C	20 - 45 mins	30 mins - 1 hour
Just starting to firm, tender	125 degrees F 52 degrees C	20 - 45 mins	30 mins - 1 hour
Milky white, firm	130 degrees F 54 degrees C	20 - 45 mins	30 mins - 1 hour

TO FINISH:

Always sear before serving and topping with a sauce. To sear, preheat a skillet over high heat until smoking. Add ghee, salted butter, or extra virgin olive oil and sear on both sides for no more than 30 seconds, until golden brown.

STEAK

"Well done doesn't always mean good job."

— *Eric Cole*
(this author's husband)

Look for meat labeled "fajita cut", "steak bites", "stew meat", etc. or just use scraps from your own trimmings. This is a great way to use extra pieces from high quality cuts.

I like to do these at 128 degrees F for 2 hours (2-3 hours from frozen). Small pieces = more surface area when searing = more opportunity to accidentally overcook, so I keep them rare!

RESULT	TEMP	TIME	TIME (FROZEN)
Rare	125 degrees F 52 degrees C	1 - 3 hours	2 - 3 hours
Medium Rare	130 degrees F 54 degrees C	1 - 4 hours	2 - 4 hours
Medium	135 degrees F 57 degrees C	1 - 4 hours	2 - 4 hours
Well Done	140 degrees F 60 degrees C	1 - 4 hours	2 - 4 hours

TO FINISH:

Always sear before topping with a sauce and serving. After sous viding, remove from the bag and pat completely dry with paper towels or a clean dish towel. To sear, preheat a skillet over high heat until smoking. Add butter or ghee and sear on both sides for no more than 1 minute, until dark brown and crusty.

Flank steak is one of my favorite cuts. I love the way it absorbs flavor, I love the texture, I love the way it's served. Frankly, I feel like flank steak doesn't get enough credit!

My favorite time and temp for flank steak is 129 degrees F for 2 hours (2-3 if cooking from frozen).

PAIR IT WITH:

GOCHUJANG COCONUT MILK MARINADE	PG 59
FAJITA MARINADE	PG 61
BLACK PEPPER ROSEMARY MARINADE	PG 63
THAI INSPIRED BASIL MARINADE	PG 65
THE EVERYTHING MARINADE	PG 67
MISO MARINADE	PG 73
GARLIC BUTTER SAUCE	PG 79
FRENCH ONION SAUCE	PG 85
BROWN SUGAR MUSTARD SAUCE	PG 89
SWEET ONION BACON SAUCE	PG 91
DILL HORSERADISH SAUCE	PG 95
BALSAMIC STRAWBERRY SALSA	PG 105

RESULT	TEMP	TIME	TIME (FROZEN)
Rare	125 degrees F 52 degrees C	1 - 3 hours	2 - 3 hours
Medium Rare	130 degrees F 54 degrees C	1 - 4 hours	2 - 4 hours
Medium	135 degrees F 57 degrees C	1 - 4 hours	2 - 4 hours
Well Done	140 degrees F 60 degrees C	1 - 4 hours	2 - 4 hours

TO FINISH:

Always sear before topping with a sauce and serving. After sous viding, remove from the bag and pat completely dry with paper towels or a clean dish towel. To sear, preheat a skillet over high heat until smoking. Add butter or ghee and sear on both sides for no more than 1 minute, until dark brown and crusty.

Slice into strips against the grain before topping with a sauce and searing.

LEAN STEAK

PAIR IT WITH:

Lean cuts will have little visible fat. These cuts include anything with "round" in the name and sirloin cuts. Strip cuts tend to be right in between lean and fatty, so eyeball the cut for visible fat and pick your route. Filet mignon is pretty lean, too!

I like to cook lean steak on the rare side at 129 degrees F for 2 hours (2-3 hours from frozen).

BLACK PEPPER ROSEMARY MARINADE	PG 63
THE EVERYTHING MARINADE	PG 67
MISO MARINADE	PG 73
GARLIC BUTTER SAUCE	PG 79
FRENCH ONION SAUCE	PG 85
BROWN SUGAR MUSTARD SAUCE	PG 89
SWEET ONION BACON SAUCE	PG 91
DILL HORSERADISH SAUCE	PG 95

RESULT	TEMP	TIME	TIME (FROZEN)
Rare	125 degrees F 52 degrees C	1 – 3 hours	2 – 3 hours
Medium Rare	130 degrees F 54 degrees C	1 – 4 hours	2 – 4 hours
Medium	135 degrees F 57 degrees C	1 – 4 hours	2 – 4 hours
Well Done	140 degrees F 60 degrees C	1 – 4 hours	2 – 4 hours

TO FINISH:

Always sear before topping with a sauce and serving. After sous viding, remove from the bag and pat completely dry with paper towels or a clean dish towel. To sear, preheat a skillet over high heat until smoking. Add salted butter or ghee and sear on both sides for no more than 1 minute, until dark brown and crusty.

FATTY STEAK

You can look at a cut to know if it's "fatty": if there are wide, visible pieces of fat on the edges and through the steak, it's fatty! Fatty cuts include ribeye, t-bone, and more.

I like to cook fatty steak at a slightly higher temp to better render the fat: 132 degrees F for 2 hours (2-3 hours if frozen).

PAIR IT WITH:

BLACK PEPPER ROSEMARY MARINADE	PG 63
THE EVERYTHING MARINADE	PG 67
GARLIC BUTTER SAUCE	PG 79
FRENCH ONION SAUCE	PG 85
BROWN SUGAR MUSTARD SAUCE	PG 89
SWEET ONION BACON SAUCE	PG 91
DILL HORSERADISH SAUCE	PG 95

RESULT	TEMP	TIME	TIME (FROZEN)
Rare	125 degrees F / 52 degrees C	1 - 3 hours	2 - 3 hours
Medium Rare	130 degrees F / 54 degrees C	1 - 4 hours	2 - 4 hours
Medium	135 degrees F / 57 degrees C	1 - 4 hours	2 - 4 hours
Well Done	140 degrees F / 60 degrees C	1 - 4 hours	2 - 4 hours

TO FINISH:

Always sear before topping with a sauce and serving. After sous viding, remove from the bag and pat completely dry with paper towels or a clean dish towel. To sear, preheat a skillet over high heat until smoking. Add butter or ghee and sear on both sides for no more than 1 minute, until dark brown and crusty.

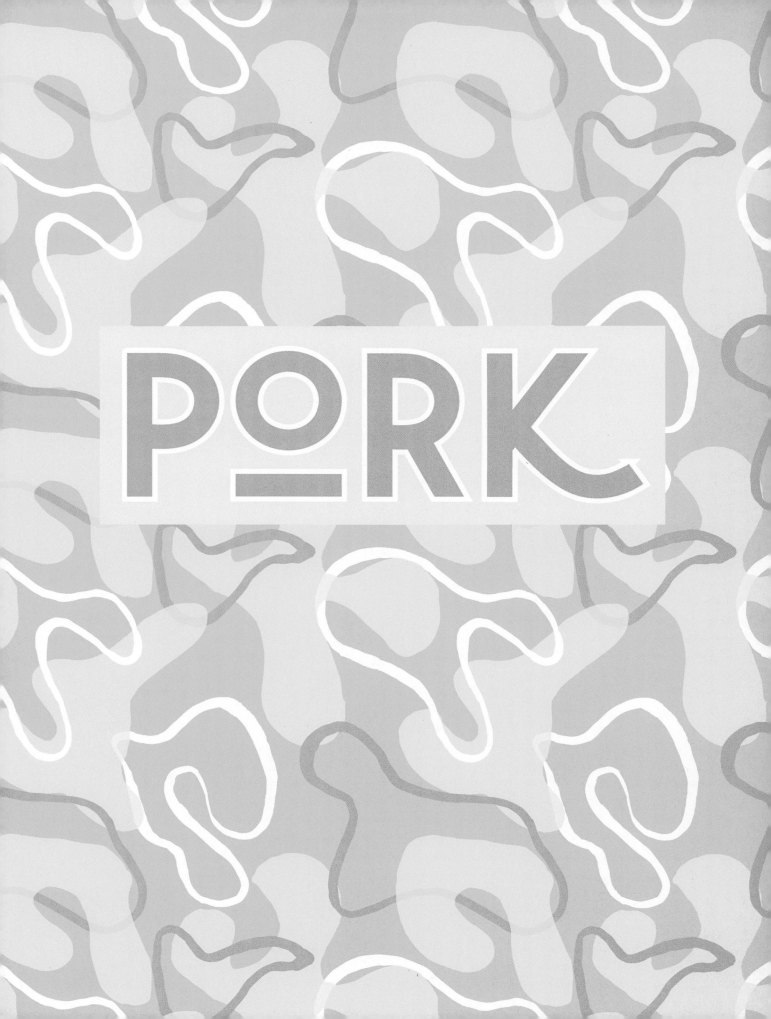

PORK CHOPS

Whenever people ask, "What's your favorite thing to sous vide?" it's a hard question to answer but pork chops always pop to mind. Pork chops have a bad reputation, but try sous viding them and you'll never look back!

I like them cooked medium, with just a bit of pink inside, so I cook them at 145 degrees F for 2 hours (2-3 hours if frozen).

RESULT	TEMP	TIME	TIME (FROZEN)
Rare (a little squeaky)	130 degrees F 54 degrees C	1 - 4 hours	2 - 4 hours
Medium Rare (juicy, meaty, tender)	135-140 degrees F 57-60 degrees C	1 - 4 hours	2 - 4 hours
Medium (firm, meaty, but still juicy)	145 degrees F 63 degrees C	1 - 4 hours	2 - 4 hours
Medium Well (completely firm, starting to dry out)	150 degrees F 65 degrees C	1 - 4 hours	2 - 4 hours

TO FINISH:

Always sear before topping with a sauce and serving. After sous viding, remove from the bag and pat completely dry with paper towels or a clean dish towel. To sear, preheat a skillet over high heat until smoking. Add butter, ghee, or olive oil and sear on both sides for no more than 1 minute, until brown and crusty.

PORK TENDERLOIN

Pork tenderloin is a great way to elevate a meal with very little effort! I love to keep a few seasoned and ready to go in the freezer in case of last minute company or if we feel like a date night in.

I like tenderloin to have just a bit of pink inside: 145 degrees F for 2 hours (2-3 hours if frozen).

RESULT	TEMP	TIME	TIME (FROZEN)
Rare (a little squeaky)	130 degrees F 54 degrees C	1 - 4 hours	2 - 4 hours
Medium Rare (juicy, meaty, tender)	135-140 degrees F 57-60 degrees C	1 - 4 hours	2 - 4 hours
Medium (firm, meaty, but still juicy)	145 degrees F 63 degrees C	1 - 4 hours	2 - 4 hours
Medium Well (completely firm, starting to dry out)	150 degrees F 65 degrees C	1 - 4 hours	2 - 4 hours

TO FINISH:

After sous viding, remove from the bag and pat completely dry with paper towels or a clean dish towel.

TO SEAR: Preheat a skillet over high heat until smoking. Add butter or olive oil and sear on all sides for no more than 30 seconds, until golden brown.

TO BROIL: Line a rimmed baking sheet with foil. Preheat your oven's broiler to high. Add tenderloin to sheet and broil until browned, about 5 minutes depending on your broiler.

PORK SHOULDER

I love sous vide for pork shoulder, especially versus the slow cooker, because you can get that incredible shreddy texture without drying it out. If you have one, I love to finish my pork shoudler on the smoker!

My favorite time and temp are 165 degrees F for 24 hours for the shreddiest, most fall apart pork shoulder possible.

RESULT	TEMP	TIME	TIME (FROZEN)
Sliceable, meaty texture	145 degrees F 63 degrees C	18 - 24 hours	20 - 24 hours
Shreddy, traditional texture	165 degrees F 74 degrees C	18 - 24 hours	20 - 24 hours

TO FINISH:

I like to crisp my pork shoulder before serving. First, shred the pork shoulder using two forks (tip: do this on a cutting board that can catch juices). Then heat a large skillet over medium-high heat.

Once hot, add the pork shoulder and toss with tongs every minute or so to crisp it up. You don't want the pan to be too crowded, so you may need to do this in batches. I also like to sprinkle salt while doing this to really enhance the flavor.

If you have a smoker, finish it on there! I like to smoke at 180 degrees F for about 4 hours.

RUBS

AN ODE TO SALT & PEPPER

While I'm about to share several delicious rubs that I encourage you to try, if you find yourself in a rush after getting home from the grocery store or just want a few options in your freezer that are seasoned simply, stick to the basics: salt and pepper.

If you sprinkle on a generous amount of S&P, you can still go from freezer to water bath and make something delicious.

But hey, for a little spice in our lives, let's get to the rubs!

BBQ RUB

1/3 cup brown sugar
2 tbsp smoked paprika
1 tbsp kosher salt
1 tbsp garlic powder
1 tbsp toasted onion powder
1 tbsp chili powder
2 tsp ground black pepper
1 tsp cayenne pepper
(optional)

Note: Sub with onion powder
if you can't find toasted, , but
toasted is worth the search!

HERB RUB

1 tbsp garlic powder
1 tbsp onion powder
1 tbsp dried oregano
1 tbsp dried thyme
1 tbsp kosher salt
1 tsp dried sage

SPICY RUB

2 tbsp smoked paprika
1 tbsp kosher salt
1 tbsp chili powder
1 tbsp garlic powder
1 tsp onion powder
1 tsp dried oregano
1 tsp cayenne pepper
½ tsp ground black pepper
½ tsp ground cloves

ZESTY RUB

1 tbsp garlic powder
1 tbsp lemon pepper
1 tbsp ground ginger
1 tbsp kosher salt
2 tsp ground cumin
1 tsp cayenne pepper
(optional)

DIRECTIONS

1. In a small, airtight container, combine all ingredients.

2. Season your protein of choice liberally with the rub. Vacuum seal and freeze until ready to cook.

MARINADES

GOCHUJANG COCONUT MILK
MARINADE & SAUCE

ENOUGH FOR 1-1.5 LBS MEAT

I love gochujang. I love its distinct spiciness. I love it mixed with plenty of coconut milk and ginger to balance out the heat. I just really love it. This marinade is excellent with a wide variety of proteins, but I tend to pair it with chicken thighs most often. I serve it simply with plenty of the sauce over rice and a steamed veg, like broccoli.

PAIR IT WITH:

☐ CHICKEN BREASTS — PG 33
☐ CHICKEN THIGHS — PG 34
☐ WHOLE CHICKEN — PG 35
☐ CHICKEN/TURKEY MEATBALLS — PG 36

☐ SALMON — PG 39
☐ WHITE FISH — PG 40
☐ SHRIMP — PG 41
☐ SCALLOPS — PG 42

☐ STEAK BITES/STRIPS — PG 45
☐ FLANK STEAK — PG 46
☐ LEAN STEAK — PG 47
☐ FATTY STEAK — PG 48

☐ PORK CHOPS — PG 51
☐ PORK TENDERLOIN — PG 52
☐ PORK SHOULDER — PG 53

YOU'LL NEED:

½ cup full fat coconut milk
2 tbsp gochujang
1 1-inch piece of ginger, peeled and grated
1 tsp garlic powder
½ tsp salt
½ tsp black pepper

½ tsp onion powder
¼ tsp cumin

1 tbsp coconut oil

1. Whisk together all ingredients except coconut oil. Add to a freezer-safe zipper top or chamber vacuum seal bag.

2. Add protein of your choice to the bag. Squish the contents to completely coat the protein. Remove the air and seal using your method of choice.

3. At this point, you can freeze and cook later or cook after 2-24 hours of marinating in the fridge.

4. When ready to cook, follow the cook time and temp instructions for your selected protein.

5. When done cooking, remove the meat from the bag. Keep the liquid in the bag.

6. Pat protein completely dry using paper towels or a clean dish towel. Heat a cast iron skillet over high heat until smoking hot. Add coconut oil to the skillet and sear the protein on all sides. Transfer to a serving plate and keep warm.

7. Add the liquid from the bag to the cast iron skillet and simmer to reduce, about 3-5 minutes. Once thickened, toss protein in the sauce or spoon over the top and serve.

   NOTE: For shrimp, you don't need to sear. Add the cooked shrimp to the cast iron skillet after you've reduced the sauce and toss to coat.

FAJ_TA
MARINADE

ENOUGH FOR I-I.5 LBS MEAT

You're going to read this recipe and be skeptical. "Protein and veggies in the same bag? How?" It totally works, I swear! This classic fajita marinade is great paired with steak, shrimp, and chicken. Serve with warm corn tortillas or in a rice bowl with plenty of diced avocado and salsa and a few extra lime wedges.

PAIR IT WITH:

■ CHICKEN BREASTS	PG 33
■ CHICKEN THIGHS	PG 34
□ WHOLE CHICKEN	PG 35
□ CHICKEN/TURKEY MEATBALLS	PG 36
□ SALMON	PG 39
□ WHITE FISH	PG 40
■ SHRIMP	PG 41
□ SCALLOPS	PG 42
■ STEAK BITES/STRIPS	PG 45
■ FLANK STEAK	PG 46
□ LEAN STEAK	PG 47
□ FATTY STEAK	PG 48
□ PORK CHOPS	PG 51
□ PORK TENDERLOIN	PG 52
■ PORK SHOULDER	PG 53

YOU'LL NEED:

MARINADE:
1 tbsp honey
1 tbsp lime juice (about ½ lime)
1 tbsp extra virgin olive oil
2 tsp Worcestershire sauce
1 tbsp chili powder
1 tsp kosher salt
1 tsp garlic powder
1 tsp onion powder
½ tsp freshly cracked black pepper
½ tsp paprika (hot or regular)
½ tsp ground cumin

VEGGIES:
1 medium red bell pepper, seeded and ribs removed, cut into thin strips
1 medium orange bell pepper, seeded and ribs removed, cut into thin strips
½ medium yellow onion, cut into thin strips

High heat cooking spray, such as canola or vegetable oil

1. Slice your protein of choice into 1-inch strips. If using shrimp, you don't need to slice.

2. Whisk together all marinade ingredients. Add mixture to a freezer-safe zipper top or chamber vacuum seal bag.

3. Add protein, bell peppers, and onions to the bag. Squish the contents to completely coat. Remove the air and seal using your method of choice.

4. At this point, you can freeze and cook later or cook after 2-24 hours of marinating in the fridge.

5. When ready to cook, follow the cook time and temp instructions for your selected protein.

6. After sous viding, preheat a cast iron skillet until it's smoking. Grease with nonstick cooking spray. Use tongs to remove protein and veggies from bag and add to skillet. Cook, tossing occasionally with tongs, until charred.

7. If desired, toss the charred protein in bag juices for extra fajita "sauce".

BLACK PEPPER ROSEMARY MARINADE

ENOUGH FOR 1-1.5 LBS MEAT

This marinade is a consistent home run and quickly became a staple around my house. Any protein marinated in this is a great addition to a big salad: Use a little of the juices from the bag as a salad dressing, lime, mint, cilantro, scallions, and tomatoes. It also pairs well with sous vide corn on the cob, found on page 143.

PAIR IT WITH:

YOU'LL NEED:

½ cup soy sauce
2 tbsp extra virgin olive oil
2 tbsp minced fresh rosemary
1 tbsp paprika
1 tbsp chili powder
1 tbsp garlic powder

2 tsp dried oregano
1 ½ tsp freshly cracked black pepper
½ tsp kosher salt

1. Whisk together all ingredients. Add to a freezer-safe zipper top or chamber vacuum seal bag.

2. Add protein of your choice to the bag. Squish the contents to completely coat the protein. Remove the air and seal using your method of choice.

3. At this point, you can freeze and cook later or cook after 2-24 hours of marinating in the fridge.

4. When ready to cook, follow the cook time and temp instructions for your selected protein.

5. When done cooking, remove the meat from the bag and finish according to instructions for your selected protein if desired.

THAI-INSPIRED BASIL
MARINADE

ENOUGH FOR 1-1.5 LBS MEAT

This marinade may have a short ingredient list, but it packs a ton of flavor. You'll want to hang on to the liquid in the bag and spoon it over your protein to get as much of that flavor as possible. Serve with rice and veggies or add to a salad for a delicious meal.

PAIR IT WITH:

☐ CHICKEN BREASTS	PG 33
☐ CHICKEN THIGHS	PG 34
☐ WHOLE CHICKEN	PG 35
☐ CHICKEN/TURKEY MEATBALLS	PG 36
☐ SALMON	PG 39
☐ WHITE FISH	PG 40
☐ SHRIMP	PG 41
☐ SCALLOPS	PG 42
☐ STEAK BITES/STRIPS	PG 45
☐ FLANK STEAK	PG 46
☐ LEAN STEAK	PG 47
☐ FATTY STEAK	PG 48
☐ PORK CHOPS	PG 51
☐ PORK TENDERLOIN	PG 52
☐ PORK SHOULDER	PG 53

YOU'LL NEED:

2 tbsp soy sauce
1 tbsp fish sauce
2 tsp garlic powder
1 tsp crushed red pepper
1 cup whole fresh Thai or regular basil leaves

1. Whisk together all ingredients except basil leaves and coconut oil. Add to a freezer-safe zipper top or chamber vacuum seal bag.

2. Add protein of your choice to the bag. Squish and toss to completely coat the protein. Add the basil and evenly distribute throughout the bag. Remove the air and seal using your method of choice.

3. At this point, you can freeze and cook later or cook after 2-24 hours of marinating in the fridge.

4. When ready to cook, follow the cook time and temp instructions for your selected protein.

5. When done cooking, remove the meat from the bag and finish according to instructions for your selected protein if desired. Keep the liquid in the bag.

6. Toss protein in the liquid from the bag or spoon over the top and serve.

THE EVERYTHING
MARINADE & SAUCE

ENOUGH FOR 1-1.5 LBS MEAT

I mean it when I say this is an everything marinade. Anything you marinate in this will taste amazing! If I happen to get a variety of proteins on sale, I love to quadruple this recipe and use it for all of the proteins I buy. Toss it in the freezer and you'll have fantastically seasoned meat at the ready! The juices from the bag make a great pan sauce with the addition of a little butter.

YOU'LL NEED:

¼ cup soy sauce
1 tbsp extra virgin olive oil
1 tbsp fresh lemon juice (about ¼ lemon)
1 tbsp Worcestershire sauce
1 tbsp Dijon mustard
1 tbsp light brown sugar
1 tbsp garlic powder

2 tsp dried basil
2 tsp dried oregano
1 tsp crushed red pepper
½ tsp kosher salt
¼ tsp freshly cracked black pepper

2 tbsp salted butter, divided

1. Whisk together all ingredients except butter. Add mixture to a freezer-safe zipper top or chamber vacuum seal bag.

2. Add protein of your choice to the bag. Squish the contents to completely coat the protein. Remove the air and seal using your method of choice.

3. At this point, you can freeze and cook later or cook after 2-24 hours of marinating in the fridge.

4. When ready to cook, follow the cook time and temp instructions for your selected protein.

5. When done cooking, remove the meat from the bag. Keep the liquid in the bag.

6. Pat the protein completely dry using paper towels or a clean dish towel. Heat a cast iron skillet over high heat until smoking hot. Add 1 tbsp of the butter to the skillet and sear the meat on all sides. Transfer to a serving plate and keep warm.

7. Add the liquid from the bag to the cast iron skillet and simmer to reduce, about 3-5 minutes. Add the remaining 1 tbsp butter to the sauce and stir until the butter is melted. Once thickened, toss protein in the sauce or spoon over the top and serve.

NOTE: For shrimp, you don't need to sear. Add the cooked shrimp to the cast iron skillet after you've made the sauce and toss to coat.

CLASSIC LEMONY
MARINADE

ENOUGH FOR 1-1.5 LBS MEAT

This lemon marinade is a classic and is amazing with chicken breasts and shrimp (but it's great on so much more!). Feel free to play with the herbs used here, but if freezing, I recommend using dried herbs over fresh herbs.

PAIR IT WITH:

■ CHICKEN BREASTS	PG 33
■ CHICKEN THIGHS	PG 34
■ WHOLE CHICKEN	PG 35
□ CHICKEN/TURKEY MEATBALLS	PG 36
■ SALMON	PG 39
■ WHITE FISH	PG 40
■ SHRIMP	PG 41
■ SCALLOPS	PG 42
□ STEAK BITES/STRIPS	PG 45
□ FLANK STEAK	PG 46
□ LEAN STEAK	PG 47
□ FATTY STEAK	PG 48
■ PORK CHOPS	PG 51
■ PORK TENDERLOIN	PG 52
□ PORK SHOULDER	PG 53

YOU'LL NEED:

¼ cup fresh lemon juice (about 1 lemon)
2 tbsp extra virgin olive oil
2 tsp garlic powder
1 tsp dried oregano
1 tsp dried parsley
1 tsp dried basil
½ tsp dried sage
½ tsp kosher salt

1. Whisk together all ingredients. Add to a freezer-safe zipper top or chamber vacuum seal bag.

2. Add protein of your choice to the bag. Squish the contents to completely coat the protein. Remove the air and seal using your method of choice.

3. At this point, you can freeze and cook later or cook after 2-24 hours of marinating in the fridge.

4. When ready to cook, follow the cook time and temp instructions for your selected protein.

5. When done cooking, remove the meat from the bag and finish according to instructions for your selected protein if desired.

CHIPOTLE MUSTARD
MARINADE & SAUCE

ENOUGH FOR 1-1.5 LBS MEAT

This recipe is for my friends who love a smoky, spicy (I'm talkin' HOT) sauce. In many ways this is just a suped up BBQ sauce but it's... *zestier* thanks to a hit of lime juice and the chipotles in adobo, which make it so delightfully smoky and spicy.

PAIR IT WITH:

■ CHICKEN BREASTS	PG 33
■ CHICKEN THIGHS	PG 34
■ WHOLE CHICKEN	PG 35
■ CHICKEN/TURKEY MEATBALLS	PG 36
□ SALMON	PG 39
□ WHITE FISH	PG 40
■ SHRIMP	PG 41
□ SCALLOPS	PG 42
□ STEAK BITES/STRIPS	PG 45
□ FLANK STEAK	PG 46
□ LEAN STEAK	PG 47
□ FATTY STEAK	PG 48
■ PORK CHOPS	PG 51
□ PORK TENDERLOIN	PG 52
■ PORK SHOULDER	PG 53

YOU'LL NEED:

¼ cup store bought barbecue sauce
¼ cup packed dark brown sugar
2 tbsp fresh lime juice (about 1 lime)
2 tbsp Dijon mustard
2-3 chipotle peppers in adobo (depending on how much spice you like)
1 tbsp sauce from can of chipotles in adobo
6 cloves of garlic
1 tsp kosher salt

1. Add all ingredients to a food processor and blend until smooth.

2. Add mixture to a freezer-safe zipper top or chamber vacuum seal bag.

3. Add protein of your choice to the bag. Squish the contents to completely coat the protein. Remove the air and seal using your method of choice.

4. At this point, you can freeze and cook later or cook after 2-24 hours of marinating in the fridge.

5. When ready to cook, follow the cook time and temp instructions for your selected protein.

6. When done cooking, remove the meat from the bag and finish according to instructions for your selected protein if desired. Place on a serving platter.

7. Toss protein in the sauce in the bag or spoon over the top and serve.

NOTE: This sauce can also be made and tossed with the protein after sous viding.

MISO
MARINADE

ENOUGH FOR 1-1.5 LBS MEAT

I'm a big fan of miso. It's incredible that just one ingredient can add so much flavor! Although miso marinades like this are most commonly used with seafood, this one is fantastic with chicken, pork, and lean steak cuts like flank steak. My favorite way to serve this is with white rice and garlicky sautéed bok choy.

PAIR IT WITH:

- ■ CHICKEN BREASTS — PG 33
- ■ CHICKEN THIGHS — PG 34
- □ WHOLE CHICKEN — PG 35
- ■ CHICKEN/TURKEY MEATBALLS — PG 36

- ■ SALMON — PG 39
- ■ WHITE FISH — PG 40
- ■ SHRIMP — PG 41
- ■ SCALLOPS — PG 42

- ■ STEAK BITES/STRIPS — PG 45
- ■ FLANK STEAK — PG 46
- ■ LEAN STEAK — PG 47
- □ FATTY STEAK — PG 48

- □ PORK CHOPS — PG 51
- □ PORK TENDERLOIN — PG 52
- □ PORK SHOULDER — PG 53

YOU'LL NEED:

¼ cup packed light brown sugar
¼ cup mirin
¼ cup white miso paste

1. Whisk together all ingredients. Add to a freezer-safe zipper top or chamber vacuum seal bag.

2. Add protein of your choice to the bag. Squish the contents to completely coat the protein. Remove the air and seal using your method of choice.

3. At this point, you can freeze and cook later or cook after 2-24 hours of marinating in the fridge.

4. When ready to cook, follow the cook time and temp instructions for your selected protein.

5. When done sous viding, move the highest oven rack in your oven to be about 4 inches from the broiler. Preheat the broiler to high. Line a rimmed baking sheet with foil.

6. Place protein on the foil lined baking sheet (if using fish, skin side should be down). Pour the contents of the bag over protein.

7. Broil for 3-5 minutes, until the top is browned. All broilers vary a bit, so keep a close eye while broiling to avoid burning.

CITRUS
MARINADE

ENOUGH FOR 1-1.5 LBS MEAT

I love a good citrusy marinade - it always comes in handy for proteins like pork, chicken, and seafood. This take is a little different than what you might be thinking (see Classic Lemony Marinade on page 69 for that!) with the additions of soy sauce and ponzu. Ponzu sauce should be in your grocery store near the soy sauce, otherwise you can find it online.

YOU'LL NEED:

¼ cup soy sauce
¼ cup fresh orange juice (about 1 orange)
2 tbsp fresh lime juice (about 1 lime)
2 tbsp fresh lemon juice (about ½ lemon)
1 tbsp extra virgin olive oil
1 tbsp ponzu

1 tsp kosher salt
1 tsp crushed red pepper
1 tsp garlic powder

1. Whisk together all ingredients. Add to a freezer-safe zipper top or chamber vacuum seal bag.

2. Add protein of your choice to the bag. Squish the contents to completely coat the protein. Remove the air and seal using your method of choice.

3. At this point, you can freeze and cook later or cook after 2-24 hours of marinating in the fridge.

4. When ready to cook, follow the cook time and temp instructions for your selected protein.

5. When done cooking, remove the meat from the bag and finish according to instructions for your selected protein if desired.

SAUCES

GARLIC BUTTER
SAUCE

ENOUGH FOR 1-1.5 LBS MEAT

With the title "Garlic Butter Sauce," this recipe doesn't need much of an introduction (or persuasion, for that matter). With the addition of soy sauce and Worcestershire sauce, it can stand up to heavier proteins like a thick steak while still being the perfect accompaniment for shrimp and scallops. For the sides, keep things classic. I recommend fluffy mashed potatoes and the Garlic Butter Green Beans on page 137.

PAIR IT WITH:

- CHICKEN BREASTS — PG 33
- CHICKEN THIGHS — PG 34
- WHOLE CHICKEN — PG 35
- CHICKEN/TURKEY MEATBALLS — PG 36

- SALMON — PG 39
- WHITE FISH — PG 40
- SHRIMP — PG 41
- SCALLOPS — PG 42

- STEAK BITES/STRIPS — PG 45
- FLANK STEAK — PG 46
- LEAN STEAK — PG 47
- FATTY STEAK — PG 48

- PORK CHOPS — PG 51
- PORK TENDERLOIN — PG 52
- PORK SHOULDER — PG 53

YOU'LL NEED:

1 tbsp + ¼ cup salted butter, separated
5 garlic cloves, minced
1 tsp soy sauce
1 tsp Worcestershire sauce
½ tsp freshly cracked black pepper
¼ cup parsley, chopped

1. Sous vide your seasoned protein of choice according to instructions.

2. After the protein is done cooking, pat protein completely dry with paper towels or a clean dish towel.

3. Preheat a cast iron skillet over medium-high heat. When the skillet is smoking, add 1 tbsp butter. Sear your protein on all sides. Set protein aside on a plate or cutting board.

4. Reduce heat to low. Add remaining ¼ cup butter and minced garlic cloves. Cook until garlic is fragrant, stirring constantly, about 1 minute. Turn off heat and add soy sauce, Worcestershire sauce, pepper, and parsley.

5. If the protein is bite-sized, toss the protein in the sauce. For all other proteins, pour sauce over the protein. Serve.

   NOTE: For shrimp, you don't need to sear. Add the cooked shrimp to the cast iron skillet after you've made the sauce and toss to coat.

FIRECRACKER PINEAPPLE SAUCE

ENOUGH FOR 1-1.5 LBS MEAT

This recipe is one of the simplest crowd pleasers while also being a go-to for me for lunches. Pile it on top of rice with some veggies or a salad or take it to the next level and make some really good spring rolls. When served with turkey or chicken meatballs, this recipe is a great appetizer. She's versatile, people!

YOU'LL NEED:

½ cup sweet hot chili sauce (such as Mae Ploy)
¼ cup drained canned pineapple tidbits
½ tsp garlic powder
½ tsp onion powder
½ tsp kosher salt
¼ tsp freshly cracked black pepper

1. Mix together all ingredients. Add to a freezer-safe zipper top or chamber vacuum seal bag.

2. Add protein of your choice to the bag. Squish the contents to completely coat the protein. Remove the air and seal using your method of choice.

3. At this point, you can freeze the meal or cook immediately.

4. When ready to sous vide, follow the cook instructions for your selected protein.

5. When done cooking, remove the meat from the bag and place on a serving platter. Pour bag juices over the protein and serve.

NOTE: This sauce can also be made and tossed with the protein after sous viding. Simply mix together all the ingredients then spoon over the top of sous vided and finished proteins.

ORANGE HARISSA HONEY GLAZE

ENOUGH FOR 1-1.5 LBS MEAT

This glaze is a show stopper. It's got a unique combination of ingredients that make it super fun and will definitely lead to a moment of silence from those who eat it. Don't skip out on the gremolata: it really makes the dish!

PAIR IT WITH:

- ■ CHICKEN BREASTS — PG 33
- ■ CHICKEN THIGHS — PG 34
- ■ WHOLE CHICKEN — PG 35
- ☐ CHICKEN/TURKEY MEATBALLS — PG 36

- ■ SALMON — PG 39
- ■ WHITE FISH — PG 40
- ■ SHRIMP — PG 41
- ■ SCALLOPS — PG 42

- ☐ STEAK BITES/STRIPS — PG 45
- ☐ FLANK STEAK — PG 46
- ☐ LEAN STEAK — PG 47
- ☐ FATTY STEAK — PG 48

- ■ PORK CHOPS — PG 51
- ■ PORK TENDERLOIN — PG 52
- ☐ PORK SHOULDER — PG 53

YOU'LL NEED:

GLAZE:
¼ cup harissa sauce (such as Trader Joe's)
¼ cup fresh orange juice (about 1 orange)
2 tbsp honey
1 tbsp salted butter, melted
½ tsp kosher salt

GREMOLATA:
¼ cup parsley, chopped
4 garlic cloves, minced
½ tsp kosher salt
Zest of 1 orange

1. Sous vide your seasoned protein of choice according to its instructions.

2. In a medium bowl, mix together all glaze ingredients.

3. In a small bowl, mix together all ingredients for the gremolata.

4. For all proteins except shrimp: Preheat your oven's broiler to high. Line a rimmed baking sheet with foil. Brush the glaze all over the protein and broil under high heat for 3-5 minutes on each side.

5. For shrimp: toss the shrimp in about half the sauce. Cook in a saute pan, tossing occasionally, over high heat for 2-3 minutes.

6. Toss protein with remaining glaze or spoon over the top. Top with gremolata and serve immediately.

FRENCH ONION SAUCE

ENOUGH FOR 1-1.5 LBS MEAT

I dreamt up this recipe with inspiration from my brother, who loves French Onion Soup. I mean, who doesn't? Packed with caramelized onions and tons of umami, this recipe is great with beef but make sure to try it with chicken and pork, too.

PAIR IT WITH:

■ CHICKEN BREASTS	PG 33
■ CHICKEN THIGHS	PG 34
☐ WHOLE CHICKEN	PG 35
■ CHICKEN/TURKEY MEATBALLS	PG 36
☐ SALMON	PG 39
☐ WHITE FISH	PG 40
☐ SHRIMP	PG 41
☐ SCALLOPS	PG 42
■ STEAK BITES/STRIPS	PG 45
■ FLANK STEAK	PG 46
■ LEAN STEAK	PG 47
■ FATTY STEAK	PG 48
■ PORK CHOPS	PG 51
■ PORK TENDERLOIN	PG 52
☐ PORK SHOULDER	PG 53

YOU'LL NEED:

1 tsp kosher salt
1 tsp dried thyme
½ tsp garlic powder
¼ tsp freshly cracked black pepper
3 tbsp salted butter, divided
1 medium onion, halved and cut into thin strips

1 tsp Worcestershire sauce
1 bay leaf
½ cup beef broth

1. In a small bowl, mix together the thyme, pepper, garlic powder, and salt. Season your protein of choice with the spice mix.

2. Heat a cast iron skillet over medium heat. Melt 1 tbsp of butter and sear the protein until browned. Set aside to a plate to catch its juices.

3. Add the remaining butter and onions to the skillet. Cook, stirring occasionally, for about 25-30 minutes until onions are caramelized.

4. Add protein and juices, onions, worcestershire sauce, bay leaf, and beef broth to your bag of choice. Remove the air and seal using your method of choice.

5. At this point, you can freeze to cook later or cook immediately.

6. When ready to cook, preheat a water bath and sous vide according to the protein you're using.

7. When done, remove the protein and place on a serving platter. Pour liquid from bag and onions over the protein and serve immediately.

SPICY POMEGRANATE SAUCE

ENOUGH FOR 1-1.5 LBS MEAT

I think we don't see pomegranate sauces served often enough. I love the tartness of pomegranate and it pairs so well with proteins like pork. I took this one up a notch with a hit of crushed red pepper, but otherwise kept it very classic.

PAIR IT WITH:

■ CHICKEN BREASTS	PG 33
■ CHICKEN THIGHS	PG 34
■ WHOLE CHICKEN	PG 35
■ CHICKEN/TURKEY MEATBALLS	PG 36
☐ SALMON	PG 39
☐ WHITE FISH	PG 40
☐ SHRIMP	PG 41
☐ SCALLOPS	PG 42
☐ STEAK BITES/STRIPS	PG 45
☐ FLANK STEAK	PG 46
☐ LEAN STEAK	PG 47
☐ FATTY STEAK	PG 48
■ PORK CHOPS	PG 51
■ PORK TENDERLOIN	PG 52
☐ PORK SHOULDER	PG 53

YOU'LL NEED:

1 tsp extra virgin olive oil
3 garlic cloves, minced
½ tsp crushed red pepper
1 cup pomegranate juice
¼ cup chicken stock
¼ tsp salt

¼ tsp freshly cracked black pepper
1 tbsp cornstarch
2 tbsp cold water

1. Sous vide and finish your seasoned protein of choice according to its instructions. Transfer to a serving plate and keep warm.

2. Heat a skillet over medium-low heat. Add the olive oil, garlic, and crushed red pepper and cook until fragrant and just starting to brown, 30 seconds to 1 minute.

3. Add the pomegranate juice, chicken stock, salt, and pepper and bring to a simmer.

4. In a small bowl, mix together the cornstarch and cold water. Whisk into the pomegranate sauce. Simmer, whisking occasionally, until the sauce thickens.

5. Taste and adjust the salt and crushed red pepper to your liking.

6. Spoon over your protein and serve.

BROWN SUGAR MUSTARD SAUCE

ENOUGH FOR 1-1.5 LBS MEAT

I love the combination of sweet and tangy in this sauce. Between the brown sugar, red wine vinegar, and Dijon mustard this sauce is flavorful, fun, and tastes great with a variety of proteins.

YOU'LL NEED:

1 tbsp salted butter
3 cloves garlic, minced
½ tsp crushed red pepper
½ cup chicken stock
¼ cup packed light brown sugar
3 tbsp Dijon mustard

2 tbsp red wine vinegar
¼ tsp salt

1. Sous vide and finish your seasoned protein of choice according to its instructions. Transfer to a serving plate and keep warm.

2. Heat a skillet over medium-low heat. Add the butter, garlic, and crushed red pepper and cook until just starting to brown and fragrant, 30 seconds to 1 minute.

3. Add the chicken stock, brown sugar, Dijon mustard, red wine vinegar, and salt and whisk. Simmer, whisking occasionally, until the sauce thickens.

4. Taste and adjust the salt and crushed red pepper to your liking.

5. Spoon over your protein and serve.

SWEET ONION BACON SAUCE

ENOUGH FOR 1-1.5 LBS MEAT

Have you heard of "engagement chicken"? It's a chicken recipe that's so good, it'll make your significant other propose on the spot after you cook it for them. This should be called engagement sauce. The literal written feedback my mom gave me after trying this recipe: "So damn good it made our eyes roll into the back of our heads!!!!!" But really, would you expect anything less from a recipe called "Sweet Onion Bacon Sauce"?

PAIR IT WITH:

YOU'LL NEED:

4 strips uncooked bacon
1 medium sweet onion, halved and cut into thin strips
½ cup lager or pilsner beer or dry white wine
½ cup beef or chicken broth
2 tbsp pure maple syrup

A few dashes of hot sauce, such as Tabasco (to your liking)
¼ tsp kosher salt
¼ tsp freshly cracked black pepper

1. Sous vide your seasoned protein of choice according to its instructions.

2. In a large skillet over medium heat, cook the bacon until crisped and browned. Transfer the bacon to a paper towel lined plate. Keep the drippings in the skillet.

3. Remove your sous vided protein from the bag and pat completely dry with paper towels or a clean dish towel. Turn the heat under the skillet up to high. Once the bacon fat is hot, sear the protein on all sides until browned. Transfer to a serving plate.

4. Reduce the heat to medium-low and add the onions. Cook, stirring occasionally, until the onions have softened and are beginning to brown, about 5-7 minutes.

5. Add the beer or wine, beef or chicken broth, maple syrup, hot sauce, salt, and pepper. Whisk to combine. Increase the heat to medium-high and simmer until thickened, 2-3 minutes.

6. Taste and adjust the hot sauce to your liking. Crumble the cooked bacon and stir into sauce.

7. Spoon over sous vided protein and serve immediately.

NOTE: For shrimp, you don't need to sear. Add the cooked shrimp to the cast iron skillet after you've made the sauce and toss to coat.

FIERY PEANUT
SAUCE

PAIR IT WITH:

■ CHICKEN BREASTS	PG 33
■ CHICKEN THIGHS	PG 34
☐ WHOLE CHICKEN	PG 35
■ CHICKEN/TURKEY MEATBALLS	PG 36
☐ SALMON	PG 39
☐ WHITE FISH	PG 40
■ SHRIMP	PG 41
☐ SCALLOPS	PG 42
☐ STEAK BITES/STRIPS	PG 45
☐ FLANK STEAK	PG 46
☐ LEAN STEAK	PG 47
☐ FATTY STEAK	PG 48
■ PORK CHOPS	PG 51
☐ PORK TENDERLOIN	PG 52
☐ PORK SHOULDER	PG 53

ENOUGH FOR 1-1.5 LBS MEAT

I love peanut sauce. If I see it on a menu, it's an easy order for me. My perfect peanut sauce is creamy, bright, has a good kick and is served on lots of chicken or shrimp over rice with a generous sprinkling of peanuts and cilantro. If you're a meal prepper (if you're reading this book, I imagine you are!), this is a great recipe for getting several lunches ready for the week.

YOU'LL NEED:

1 tsp neutral oil (canola, vegetable, or grapeseed oil)
4 garlic cloves, minced
1 tbsp minced fresh ginger (about a 1-inch knob)
½ tsp crushed red pepper
½ cup warm water
½ cup peanut butter
1 tbsp lime juice (juice of about ½ lime)

1 tbsp soy sauce
1 tbsp fish sauce
1 tbsp sriracha

2 tbsp chopped fresh cilantro, for serving
2 tbsp finely chopped peanuts, for serving

1. Sous vide your seasoned protein of choice according to its instructions.

2. Heat oil in a saucepan over medium heat. Add garlic, ginger, and crushed red pepper to hot oil and cook until fragrant, about 1 minute.

3. Reduce the heat to the lowest setting possible. Add warm water, peanut butter, lime juice, soy sauce, fish sauce, and sriracha and stir until smooth.

4. Cook, stirring occasionally, at a simmer until homogenous, about 5 minutes.

5. Taste and adjust sriracha to your liking.

6. Top your cooked protein of choice with the sauce. Garnish with cilantro and peanuts.

D!LL HORSERADISH
SAUCE

ENOUGH FOR 1-1.5 LBS MEAT

Growing up, my family's go-to condiment for steak was horseradish cream. To this day, I still love it with a fatty steak like ribeye, but sometimes I go the extra mile and make a dipping sauce that's just a little fancier. It also makes a great sauce for sandwiches and wraps!

PAIR IT WITH:

☐ CHICKEN BREASTS — PG 33
☐ CHICKEN THIGHS — PG 34
☐ WHOLE CHICKEN — PG 35
☐ CHICKEN/TURKEY MEATBALLS — PG 36

☐ SALMON — PG 39
☐ WHITE FISH — PG 40
☐ SHRIMP — PG 41
☐ SCALLOPS — PG 42

☐ STEAK BITES/STRIPS — PG 45
☐ FLANK STEAK — PG 46
☐ LEAN STEAK — PG 47
☐ FATTY STEAK — PG 48

☐ PORK CHOPS — PG 51
☐ PORK TENDERLOIN — PG 52
☐ PORK SHOULDER — PG 53

YOU'LL NEED:

¼ cup Greek yogurt
¼ cup sour cream
2 tbsp chopped fresh dill
1 tbsp horseradish cream
½ tsp kosher salt
¼ tsp freshly cracked black pepper

1. Sous vide and finish your seasoned protein of choice according to its instructions.

2. Stir together all ingredients in a bowl. Taste and add more horseradish cream to make the sauce spicier if desired.

3. Spoon sauce over your protein of choice or next to for dipping and serve.

PRESTO PESTO

1 cup packed fresh basil leaves
3 cloves garlic
¼ cup grated Parmesan
¼ tsp kosher salt
¼ tsp freshly cracked black pepper
¼ cup extra virgin olive oil

1. Add basil, garlic, Parmesan, salt, and pepper in the bowl of a food processor.
2. With the motor running, slowly drizzle in the extra virgin olive oil until emulsified.

PESTO & SUN DRIED TOMATO SAUCE

ENOUGH FOR 1-1.5 LBS MEAT

Do you know what's underrated? Sun dried tomatoes. Sure, they were overused in the 80s, but that's because they're delicious! Especially when combined with pesto and lemon. I like to serve this with orzo or Parmesan Polenta (page 145) and Lemony Asparagus (page 133).

PAIR IT WITH:

■ CHICKEN BREASTS	PG 33
■ CHICKEN THIGHS	PG 34
■ WHOLE CHICKEN	PG 35
■ CHICKEN/TURKEY MEATBALLS	PG 36
■ SALMON	PG 39
■ WHITE FISH	PG 40
■ SHRIMP	PG 41
■ SCALLOPS	PG 42
☐ STEAK BITES/STRIPS	PG 45
☐ FLANK STEAK	PG 46
☐ LEAN STEAK	PG 47
☐ FATTY STEAK	PG 48
■ PORK CHOPS	PG 51
■ PORK TENDERLOIN	PG 52
☐ PORK SHOULDER	PG 53

YOU'LL NEED:

¼ cup oil packed sun dried tomatoes, drained and roughly chopped
3 tbsp pesto (store bought or recipe on page 96)
1 tsp kosher salt
4 lemon slices

1. Mix together sun dried tomatoes, pesto, and kosher salt. Add to a vacuum sealable bag.

2. Add protein of your choice to the bag. Squish and toss to completely coat the protein. Add the lemon slices and evenly distribute throughout the bag. Remove the air and seal using your method of choice.

3. At this point, you can freeze and cook later or cook after 2-24 hours of marinating in the fridge.

4. When ready to cook, follow the cook time and temp instructions for your selected protein. If desired, finish according to your protein's instructions.

5. Serve with the liquid in the bag.

NOTE: This sauce can also be made and tossed with the protein after sous viding. Mix together sun dried tomatoes, pesto, salt, and squeeze half a lemon into the sauce rather than using slices. Toss with your sous vided and finished protein or spoon over the top.

ASHLEY'S RANCH

My friend Ashley of the blog Millennial Kitchen has the best ranch recipe. There's always a container of it in my fridge! When I was coming up with recipes for this cookbook, I knew I wanted to include ranch and some fun variations. And I thought, "Why reinvent the wheel?" So, I asked Ashley if I could include her perfect recipe and she generously obliged!

ASHLEY'S RECIPE

¾ cup mayonnaise
¾ cup sour cream
¾ cup buttermilk
2 tbsp chopped parsley
1 ½ tbsp chopped chives
1 ½ tbsp chopped scallions
1 tbsp white vinegar
1 tsp kosher salt
½ tsp garlic powder
½ tsp freshly cracked black pepper

1. Whisk together all ingredients in a medium bowl. Let sit for 30 minutes before serving.
2. Store in an airtight container in the fridge.

CHECK OUT ASHLEY'S BLOG! MILLENNIAL KITCHEN

VARIATIONS

PESTO RANCH

2/3 cup Ashley's Ranch
1/4 cup Presto Pesto (pg 96)

1. Whisk together all ingredients in a medium bowl.
2. Taste and add more pesto if desired.
3. Store in an airtight container in the fridge.

HARISSA RANCH

2/3 cup Ashley's Ranch
1 tbsp harissa paste
1 tbsp fresh lemon juice

1. Whisk together all ingredients in a medium bowl.
2. Store in an airtight container in the fridge.

NOTE: Trader Joe's harissa is my favorite!

KIMCHI RANCH

2/3 cup Ashley's Ranch
1/3 cup finely chopped kimchi
1 tbsp chopped cilantro
1 tbsp sriracha

1. Whisk together all ingredients in a medium bowl.
2. Store in an airtight container in the fridge.

These ranches taste great with just about anything. Serve them as a dipping sauce or smear on top of fish or chicken before broiling.

MANGO
SALSA

ENOUGH FOR 1-1.5 LBS MEAT

Mango salsa is a great way to liven up any dish and it doesn't just have to be in a taco situation. It's delicious served over the top of an entrée with a simple veggie side, in a rice bowl, and in spring rolls. Get creative and transcend the taco! (But also, make some tacos!)

PAIR IT WITH:

- CHICKEN BREASTS — PG 33
- CHICKEN THIGHS — PG 34
- WHOLE CHICKEN — PG 35
- CHICKEN/TURKEY MEATBALLS — PG 36

- SALMON — PG 39
- WHITE FISH — PG 40
- SHRIMP — PG 41
- SCALLOPS — PG 42

- STEAK BITES/STRIPS — PG 45
- FLANK STEAK — PG 46
- LEAN STEAK — PG 47
- FATTY STEAK — PG 48

- PORK CHOPS — PG 51
- PORK TENDERLOIN — PG 52
- PORK SHOULDER — PG 53

YOU'LL NEED:

2 ripe mangos, peeled, pitted, and diced
1 medium red bell pepper, ribs and seeds removed, diced
½ red onion, diced
1 jalapeño, ribs and seeds removed, finely chopped
¼ cup chopped cilantro
1 tbsp lime juice (about ½ lime)
¼ tsp kosher salt

1. Sous vide your seasoned protein of choice according to its instructions.

2. Combine all ingredients in a bowl. Allow to sit for at least 5 minutes before serving.

3. Sear your protein according to its instructions if applicable.

4. Spoon salsa over your protein of choice and serve.

COTIJA CORN
SALSA

PAIR IT WITH:

■ CHICKEN BREASTS	PG 33
■ CHICKEN THIGHS	PG 34
■ WHOLE CHICKEN	PG 35
☐ CHICKEN/TURKEY MEATBALLS	PG 36
■ SALMON	PG 39
■ WHITE FISH	PG 40
■ SHRIMP	PG 41
■ SCALLOPS	PG 42
☐ STEAK BITES/STRIPS	PG 45
☐ FLANK STEAK	PG 46
☐ LEAN STEAK	PG 47
☐ FATTY STEAK	PG 48
■ PORK CHOPS	PG 51
☐ PORK TENDERLOIN	PG 52
☐ PORK SHOULDER	PG 53

ENOUGH FOR 1-1.5 LBS MEAT

I love this salsa - it's so fresh and absolutely screams summer. You can make it anytime of the year when you swap fresh corn for canned or frozen. Please don't skip the cotija cheese! It's what makes this salsa a little special and if you're anything like me, you'll find yourself reaching for extra cotija. I love to pair this salsa with proteins seasoned with the Spicy Rub on page 55.

YOU'LL NEED:

15.25 oz can of corn kernels or 1 ½ cups frozen or fresh corn kernels (about 2 ears)
2 roma tomatoes, deseeded and diced
½ red onion, diced
1 jalapeño, ribs and seeds removed, finely chopped

¼ cup chopped cilantro
1 tbsp lime juice (about ½ lime)
1 tbsp crumbled cotija cheese
½ tsp kosher salt

1. Sous vide your seasoned protein of choice according to its instructions.

2. If using canned kernels, drain the liquid, rinse, and pat dry with a clean dish towel. If using frozen corn kernels, rinse them under cold water to defrost and pat dry with a clean dish towel. If using fresh, the lime juice in this recipe will "cook" the corn or it's great with grilled or sous vided Corn on the Cob (page 143).

3. Combine all ingredients in a bowl. Allow to sit for at least 5 minutes before serving.

4. Sear your protein according to its instructions if applicable.

5. Spoon salsa over your protein of choice and serve.

BALSAMIC STRAWBERRY SALSA

ENOUGH FOR 1-1.5 LBS MEAT

I first tested this recipe (along with several others) on my family, and the response made me know I had a winner on my hands. The savory + sweet + vinegar flavor combination really lights up any dish. I tend to serve it with chicken most often but it's great with seafood, pork, and even flank steak, too!

PAIR IT WITH:

- CHICKEN BREASTS — PG 33
- CHICKEN THIGHS — PG 34
- WHOLE CHICKEN — PG 35
- ☐ CHICKEN/TURKEY MEATBALLS — PG 36

- SALMON — PG 39
- WHITE FISH — PG 40
- SHRIMP — PG 41
- SCALLOPS — PG 42

- ☐ STEAK BITES/STRIPS — PG 45
- FLANK STEAK — PG 46
- ☐ LEAN STEAK — PG 47
- ☐ FATTY STEAK — PG 48

- PORK CHOPS — PG 51
- PORK TENDERLOIN — PG 52
- ☐ PORK SHOULDER — PG 53

YOU'LL NEED:

1 ½ cups strawberries, hulled and diced
3 roma tomatoes, deseeded and diced
½ red onion, diced
2 tbsp balsamic vinegar
7 large basil leaves, sliced into long, thin strips

1. Sous vide your seasoned protein of choice according to its instructions.

2. Combine all ingredients in a bowl. Allow to sit for at least 5 minutes before serving.

3. Sear your protein according to its instructions if applicable.

4. Spoon salsa over your protein of choice and serve.

	BEEF	PORK/CHICKEN	SEAFOOD	VEGGIES	GRAINS
BLUE CHEESE BUTTER	✓	✓			✓
CHIPOTLE MAPLE BUTTER		✓	✓		
CURRY BUTTER		✓	✓	✓	
HABANERO CILANTRO LIME BUTTER		✓	✓	✓	
SUN DRIED TOMATO ANCHOVY BUTTER	✓	✓		✓	✓
ROSEMARY BLACK PEPPER BUTTER	✓	✓		✓	✓
SESAME SRIRACHA BUTTER	✓	✓	✓		

COMPOUND BUTTERS

CURRY

½ cup (1 stick) salted butter, softened
1 tsp ground cumin
½ tsp ground turmeric
½ tsp ground coriander
½ tsp black pepper
½ tsp ground cinnamon
¼ tsp ground cardamom
¼ tsp cayenne pepper

SUN DRIED TOMATO ANCHOVY

½ cup (1 stick) salted butter, softened
4 minced garlic cloves
4 anchovies packed in oil, drained and minced
1 tbsp sun dried tomatoes packed in oil, drained and minced
1 tsp fresh lemon juice

ROSEMARY BLACK PEPPER

½ cup (1 stick) salted butter, softened
1 tbsp finely chopped fresh rosemary (about 1 sprig)
1 ½ tsp freshly cracked black pepper
1 tsp garlic powder

BLUE CHEESE

½ cup (1 stick) salted butter, softened
¼ cup crumbled blue cheese
¼ cup packed parsley, finely chopped
2 tsp finely chopped chives
1 tsp garlic powder
¼ tsp ground black pepper

SESAME SRIRACHA

½ cup (1 stick) salted butter, softened
2 tbsp sriracha
2 tsp sesame seeds
½ tsp sesame oil

CHIPOTLE MAPLE

½ cup (1 stick) salted butter, softened
1 chipotle in adobo, finely chopped (about 1 tbsp)
1 tbsp maple syrup
¼ tsp ground black pepper

HABANERO CILANTRO LIME

½ cup (1 stick) salted butter, softened
1 habanero pepper, minced
¼ cup finely chopped cilantro
1 tbsp fresh squeezed lime juice (about half a lime)
½ tsp lime zest

DIRECTIONS

1. Add all ingredients to a bowl and mash them together with a fork until well combined but still a little chunky.

2. Spoon mixture onto a piece of parchment paper or plastic wrap, form it into a log, and wrap. Twist the ends to secure them. Alternatively, add all ingredients to a small canning jar. Freeze.

3. For all proteins except shrimp: when ready to serve, heat a cast iron skillet over high heat. When smoking, add 1 tbsp plain butter and sear on all sides. Top each serving with a pat of compound butter and allow to melt.

4. For shrimp, top with compound butter immediately after removing from bag after cooking and toss to melt the butter and coat the shrimp.

NOTES:
- If using unsalted butter, add an additional ¼ tsp salt.
- Butter can be kept frozen for up to 6 months.
- For lean proteins like fish or chicken, slices of compound butter can be added directly to bag before vacuum sealing. However, I prefer to place on top of cooked and seared proteins and allow it to melt over them.

48-HOUR
"BRAISED" SHORT RIBS
SERVES 4 TO 6

Okay, I'm going to be up front: This recipe takes a really long time to cook. REALLY. LONG. But it is so worth it! To quote Heather, one of my recipe testers: "AMAZING!!!! SO GOOD!!" And, not to toot my own horn, I absolutely agree. This dish could be made in a shorter time by braising, but sous vide creates a deeper flavor you just can't get any other way.

YOU'LL NEED:

2 ½ lbs boneless beef short ribs, cut into 2-inch pieces
Kosher salt
Freshly cracked black pepper
2 tbsp salted butter
1 shallot, finely diced
½ cup red wine
2 tbsp tomato paste
3 sprigs fresh thyme
1 dried bay leaf

FOR SERVING:
Pasta or Parmesan Polenta (pg 145)
¼ cup chopped fresh parsley

1. Preheat a water bath using an immersion circulator to 175 degrees F if cooking immediately.

2. Season the short ribs liberally with salt and pepper. Preheat a large cast iron skillet over medium-high heat. Once hot, add the butter and sear the short ribs on all sides until deep brown without crowding the skillet (this may need to be done in batches). Remove the short ribs to a plate.

3. Reduce the heat to low. Add the diced shallot and cook, stirring occasionally, for 2-3 minutes until softened. Add the red wine and stir to deglaze the pan. Add the tomato paste and stir to combine. Simmer for 3-4 minutes until reduced by about one-third.

4. Transfer the short ribs, red wine mixture, thyme, and bay leaf to a bag of your choice. Remove the air and seal using your method of choice.

5. At this point you can freeze or cook immediately.

6. When ready to cook, cook in a water bath preheated to 175 degrees F for 48 hours.

7. When finished, add the contents of the bag, including liquid, to a shallow serving bowl and shred the short ribs by inserting two forks and pulling them apart.

8. Serve with polenta or pasta and lots of freshly chopped parsley.

PIMENTO STUFFED BURGERS

SERVES 4 GENEROUSLY

If you have my first cookbook, *Everyday Sous Vide*, you know that I have an affinity for stuffed burgers. This version with store bought pimento cheese is easy to put together and a total show stopper. It's a great recipe to have ready in your freezer!

YOU'LL NEED:

FOR THE PATTIES:
2 lbs 80/20 ground beef
Kosher salt
½ cup store bought pimento cheese

FOR THE BURGERS:
1 yellow onion, thinly sliced
1 tsp extra virgin olive oil
4 brioche burger buns
8 slices cooked bacon
Pickle slices

1. If cooking immediately, preheat a water bath using an immersion circulator to 135 degrees F for medium burgers (increase temp to 145 degrees F if you prefer well done).

2. Divide the ground beef into 8 4 oz portions. Flatten them into ¼ inch thick patties. Lightly season all patties with kosher salt.

3. Add 2 tbsp pimento cheese to the center of 4 of the patties. Place the patties without pimento cheese on top of the patties with pimento cheese. Gently pinch the edges of the patties together to seal the pimento cheese inside.

4. Carefully add all the patties to a large bag of your choice in a single layer without touching. Gently remove the air (if using a vacuum sealer, use the manual setting and stop the seal as soon as the air is gone).

5. At this point, you can freeze the patties or cook immediately.

6. When ready to cook, add the bag to the preheated water bath and make sure the patties stay completely submerged (sous vide magnets or a ceramic plate work well for this). Cook for 45 minutes to 2 hours (at least 1 hour 30 minutes if cooking from frozen).

7. While the burgers are cooking, prepare the onions. In a skillet over medium high heat, add the olive oil. Add the onions and cook until the edges start to char and the onions are softened. Set aside.

8. After patties are done sous viding, remove from the bag and pat dry using paper towels or a clean dish towel. Preheat a cast iron skillet or a grill over high heat. Once hot, brown the burgers on each side, about 2 minutes.

9. Toast the buns in the same skillet or over the grill.

10. To assemble the burgers, add patties to bottom buns and top each with 2 bacon slices, a pile of onions, and pickles. Top with top buns and serve immediately.

BUTTERMILK FRIED CHICKEN

SERVES 4

You might be wondering: why sous vide chicken you're going to fry? When you sous vide first, you'll ensure the chicken is cooked through and it's far more tender than with just a deep fry. For traditional fried chicken to eat with your hands, use bone-in, skin-on chicken thighs. However, if you feel like making fried chicken sandwiches, use boneless, skinless chicken thighs.

YOU'LL NEED:

MARINADE:
1 cup buttermilk
1 tsp kosher salt
1 tsp garlic powder
1 tsp onion powder
½ tsp freshly cracked black pepper
½ tsp paprika
¼ tsp cayenne pepper (optional)

1 ½ pounds bone-in or boneless chicken thighs (about 4-6)

DREDGE:
2 large eggs
1 cup all-purpose flour
½ tsp kosher salt
½ tsp paprika
¼ tsp freshly cracked black pepper
¼ tsp cayenne pepper (optional)

High-heat oil for frying (such as canola)
Kosher salt

1. In a small bowl, whisk together all the marinade ingredients. Add the chicken to your bag of choice and pour the marinade over top. Massage the chicken with the marinade so it's completely coated. Seal the bag using your method of choice.
2. At this point, you can freeze the chicken or let it marinate in the fridge for at least 2 hours or up to 24 hours before cooking.
3. When ready to cook, preheat a water bath using an immersion circulator to 155 degrees F. Add the bag of marinated chicken to the water bath and cook for 2-4 hours.
4. While the chicken is cooking, prepare your dredging station. In a shallow bowl, whisk together the eggs. In another shallow bowl, combine the flour, salt, paprika, pepper, and cayenne pepper. Line a baking sheet with paper towels or ready a wire rack set over a paper-towel-lined baking sheet.
5. About 15 minutes before you plan to fry the chicken, add enough oil to a large, deep pot or Dutch oven to come about 3 inches up the side of the pot. Place over medium-high heat and bring to 350 degrees F. Adjust the heat to maintain the oil at that temperature.
6. Remove the chicken from the bag and shake off excess marinade. Transfer the chicken to the shallow dish with the eggs. Discard the cooking bag and its contents.
7. Turn the chicken so that it is completely coated with egg. Let the excess drip off and then coat each chicken thigh thoroughly in the seasoned flour mixture. Gently shake to remove excess flour.
8. Carefully place the chicken in the oil, frying in batches if necessary so as to not crowd the pan. Turn the chicken as needed, until the skin is golden brown on all sides, about 7 minutes.
9. Transfer the chicken to the wire rack or paper-towel-lined baking sheet. While hot from frying, sprinkle with a little kosher salt. Serve immediately.

NOTE: If you want to make a fried chicken sandwich, mix together equal parts ketchup and mayonnaise (add a little sriracha if you like things spicy!). Spread this mixture on both sides of a hamburger bun. Add the boneless, skinless fried chicken, place pickle chips on top, and serve immediately.

CHICKEN SHAWARMA

SERVES 3-4

This recipe is great for a weeknight dinner or when we have company. It tastes amazing, looks beautiful, and is easy to serve whether you go for a buffet serving situation or serve it family style. I usually don't bother searing the chicken after sous viding for the sake of simplicity, but it will look even prettier if you add color to the cooked chicken thighs.

YOU'LL NEED:

FOR THE CHICKEN:
1 pound boneless skinless chicken thighs
2 tbsp fresh lemon juice (about ½ lemon)
1 tbsp extra virgin olive oil
1 tbsp paprika
2 tsp garlic powder
1 tsp kosher salt
1 tsp ground cumin
1 tsp ground turmeric
1 tsp onion powder
½ tsp cayenne pepper

FOR THE TZATZIKI:
2 cups Greek yogurt
½ English cucumber, peeled, and finely diced
4 garlic cloves, minced
1 tbsp extra virgin olive oil
1 tsp white vinegar
½ tsp kosher salt

FOR SERVING:
¼ cup chopped parsley
4 pita breads, warmed
Lemon wedges

1. If cooking immediately, preheat a water bath using an immersion circulator to 155 degrees F, or to desired temperature from page 34.

2. Trim chicken thighs to remove any excess fat. Cut into 1-inch pieces.

3. In a small bowl, whisk together the lemon juice, extra virgin olive oil, and all the spices for the chicken.

4. Transfer the chicken and spice mixture to a bag of your choice and massage to completely coat. Remove the air and seal using your method of choice.

5. At this point, you can freeze the chicken or cook immediately.

6. When ready to cook, place in a preheated water bath and cook for 1-3 hours (2 hours minimum if cooking from frozen).

7. While the chicken is cooking, prepare the tzatziki sauce. Combine all ingredients in a medium bowl. Cover and refrigerate until ready to serve.

8. When the chicken is done, remove from the bag. Discard the bag and juices. Searing is optional. If you'd like to sear the chicken, preheat a cast iron skillet or grill pan over high heat. Add 1 tsp extra virgin olive oil and the chicken and cook until the edges are nicely browned.

9. Transfer the chicken to a platter and garnish with parsley. Serve with pita, the tzatziki sauce, and lemon wedges.

PROSCIUTTO-WRAPPED ARTICHOKE DIP
STUFFED CHICKEN BREASTS

SERVES 4-8

This is one of those recipes I dreamed up and was thrilled to discover was just as amazing in my head as it was in reality. Creamy, savory artichoke dip and salty prosciutto are balanced by blistered cherry tomatoes for a seriously delicious meal. Even though each piece consists of just one chicken breast, this is very filling and they can be sliced into rounds to feed a larger crowd.

YOU'LL NEED:

ARTICHOKE DIP:
(You can also use store bought!)
1 can water-packed artichoke hearts, drained and roughly chopped
½ cup grated Parmesan cheese
½ cup mayonnaise
½ cup sour cream
½ tsp kosher salt
½ tsp freshly cracked black pepper

CHICKEN:
4 boneless skinless chicken breasts
Kosher salt
Freshly cracked black pepper
4-8 slices of prosciutto

FINISHING:
2 tsp extra virgin olive oil
1 cup cherry tomatoes
1 tsp chopped fresh thyme leaves

1. If cooking immediately, preheat a water bath to 150 degrees F using an immersion circulator (or your preferred temperature for chicken breasts from page 33).
2. Mix together all the ingredients for the artichoke dip in a bowl. Set aside.
3. On a large cutting board, butterfly each chicken breast. Alternatively, to create smaller pieces, you can butterfly and cut all the way through, creating two pieces from each chicken breast. Arrange the chicken breasts in a single layer on the cutting board. Cover with a layer of plastic wrap. Pound the chicken breasts with a meat pounder into a ½ inch thick, even piece. Remove the plastic wrap.
4. Season the chicken lightly on both sides with salt and pepper.
5. Drop a large spoonful of the dip onto each chicken breast and spread evenly over the breast. Roll each up and then wrap with a piece of prosciutto. (A second piece of prosciutto may be required to wrap completely.)
6. Add all the rolled chicken breasts to a large bag of your choice in a single layer without touching. Gently remove the air (if using a vacuum sealer, use the manual setting and stop the seal as soon as the air is gone).
7. At this point, you can freeze the chicken or cook immediately.
8. When ready to cook, add the bag to the preheated water bath and cook for 2-4 hours.
9. When the chicken is done sous viding, remove from the bag and pat dry with paper towels or a clean dish towel.
10. Searing is optional, but if you'd like to, preheat a large skillet over medium-high heat and add the olive oil. Sear the chicken on all sides until prosciutto is just browned. Transfer to a serving plate. (As an option, you can stretch the portion size by cutting each piece crosswise into rounds.)
11. To finish the dish, reduce the heat to medium. Add more olive oil if necessary and then add the cherry tomatoes. Cook until they begin to blister and brown, about 5 minutes. Add the thyme leaves and remove from heat.
12. Top the chicken breasts with the tomatoes and thyme and serve immediately.

PIRI PIRI INSPIRED
WHOLE CHICKEN

SERVES 4-6

Piri piri is one of my favorite flavor combinations—spicy, lemony, and smoky. Don't let the relatively short ingredient list fool you: This recipe packs so much flavor! I love to serve this chicken with the Crispy Potatoes found on page 123, but no judgement if you go for heating up some frozen french fries or tater tots. This marinade freezes beautifully so if you see whole chickens on sale, buy a few and stock your freezer with chicken ready to be sous vided!

YOU'LL NEED:

1 whole chicken, spatchcocked or 2-3 lbs bone-in, skin-on chicken pieces
Kosher salt

MARINADE:
2 red serrano peppers
5 garlic cloves
¼ cup fresh lemon juice (about 1 lemon)
2 tbsp extra virgin olive oil
2 tbsp tomato paste
1 tbsp smoked paprika

TOMATO BUTTER:
4 tbsp salted butter
2 tbsp tomato paste

1. Season the chicken all over with kosher salt. Set aside.

2. Add all marinade ingredients to the bowl of a food processor and pulse until a paste is formed. Rub the paste all over the chicken, including under the skin.

3. Add the entire chicken to a large bag of your choice. Remove the air and seal using your method of choice.

4. At this point you can freeze the chicken or let marinate in the refrigerator for 2-24 hours before cooking.

5. When ready to cook, preheat a water bath using an immersion circulator to 155 degrees F. Add the bag to the preheated water bath and cook according to the chart for your size of chicken on page 35.

6. When the chicken is nearly done, melt the butter in a small saucepan over medium-low heat. Remove from the heat and stir in the tomato paste.

7. Preheat your oven's broiler to high. Line a large rimmed baking sheet with foil.

8. When the chicken is done sous viding, remove from the bag and place on the foil-lined baking sheet, skin side up. Pat dry with paper towels or a clean dish towel. Brush the skin all over with the tomato butter.

9. Broil the chicken until browned, about 5 minutes. Transfer to a cutting board and cut into pieces. Serve immediately.

PESTO TURKEY MEATBALLS
WITH WHIPPED FETA & CRISPY POTATOES

SERVES 4-6

This recipe was simply going to be "Pesto Turkey Meatballs with Whipped Feta," but I feel the crispy potatoes are essential to the meal, so they had to be included. I am also very biased towards my method of making crispy potatoes. On the face of it, this recipe may look involved, but each component (the meatballs, the potatoes, the whipped feta) is easier to prepare than you'd think. Double the meatball batch so you have extra for the freezer!

YOU'LL NEED:

TURKEY MEATBALLS:
1 lb ground turkey
½ cup Panko bread crumbs
¼ cup homemade (page 96) or store bought pesto
1 large egg
1 tsp onion powder
1 tsp kosher salt
½ tsp freshly cracked black pepper
1 tbsp salted butter

CRISPY POTATOES:
Kosher salt (for salting the water)

1 lb yellow potatoes, scrubbed and cut into 1-inch cubes
2 tbsp extra virgin olive oil
5 cloves garlic, minced
½ tsp kosher salt
½ tsp Italian seasoning
Cooking spray

WHIPPED FETA:
8 oz feta cheese, crumbled, at room temp
2 oz cream cheese, at room temp

Chopped parsley, for serving

1. In a large bowl, combine all the ingredients for the turkey meatballs except the butter. Shape into 12 meatballs.
2. Add the meatballs to a bag of your choice. Gently remove the air and seal. At this point, you can freeze the meatballs if you wish to cook at a later date.
3. When ready to cook, preheat the water bath using an immersion circulator to 150 degrees F. Add to the water bath and cook for 1-4 hours (at least 2 if cooking from frozen).
4. When the meatballs are about an hour from being done, prepare the potatoes. Preheat oven to 450 degrees F. Bring a large stockpot of water to a boil.
5. When the water is boiling, add 2 heaping spoonfuls of salt to the water. Taste the water - it should taste salty. Add more salt if necessary. Add the potatoes and boil until just fork tender, 8-10 minutes. Drain in a colander, shaking off excess water. Empty all the water from the stockpot, wiping dry with a towel if needed.
6. Add the olive oil and garlic to the stockpot. Add the potatoes, salt, and Italian seasoning. Pick the pot up by the handles and shake to coat the potatoes. Shake hard enough to beat the potatoes up - the outside of the potatoes should have a mashed potato-like consistency.
7. Spray a rimmed baking sheet with cooking spray. Add the potatoes and arrange so they aren't touching one another.
8. Bake for 15 minutes. Remove from the oven and use a spatula to flip the potatoes. Bake until completely golden brown on all sides, about 15-20 minutes longer.
9. While the meatballs and potatoes are cooking, make the whipped feta. In the bowl of a food processor fitted with the metal blade, pulse the feta until finely crumbled. Add the cream cheese and process until combined, light, and fluffy, about 2-3 minutes. Transfer to a small bowl.
10. When the meatballs are done, heat a cast iron skillet over medium-high heat. Add the butter. Sear the meatballs on all sides to brown.
11. To serve, use about 3 tbsp of the whipped feta to make a thick layer on the bottom of each dinner plate. Top with the potatoes and meatballs. Sprinkle parsley over the top and serve immediately.

CLASSIC
PORK CHOPS & APPLES

SERVES 4 GENEROUSLY

The first time you sous vide pork chops, your perception of them will completely change. Pork chops have a reputation for being dry, boring, and bland (the number of teenagers complaining when their mom serves pork chops for dinner on social media!). They don't have to be that way. This classic recipe, pairing pork and apples, is my favorite way to show off this cut's potential.

YOU'LL NEED:

2 tbsp light brown sugar
2 tbsp Dijon mustard
½ tsp kosher salt
¼ tsp ground cinnamon
4 bone-in or boneless pork chops

1 Granny Smith apple, peeled, cored, and thinly sliced
½ yellow onion, thinly sliced
2 tbsp salted butter, divided

1. If cooking immediately, preheat a water bath using an immersion circulator to your desired temperature from page 51.

2. In a small bowl, mix together the brown sugar, mustard, salt, and cinnamon. Rub the mixture all over the pork chops.

3. Add the pork chops to your bag of choice, along with the apple and onion slices. Remove the air and seal.

4. At this point you can freeze the pork chops or cook immediately.

5. When ready to cook, add to the preheated water bath and cook for 2-4 hours.

6. When done, remove the pork chops from the bag and pat them dry with a clean dish towel or paper towels. Save the bag and it's contents.

7. Place a a cast iron skillet over high heat. When hot, add 1 tbsp butter and swirl to coat the bottom of the pan. Add the pork chops and sear, turning once, until browned on both sides, about 2 minutes. Transfer to a serving plate.

8. Reduce the heat to low and add remaining butter, apples, onions, and juices from the bag to the pan. Simmer until the liquid is reduced and the apples and onions are tender and starting to brown, about 5 minutes.

9. Spoon the apple and onion mixture over the pork chops and serve immediately.

CARN!TAS

SERVES 8 TO 12

I love carnitas. Pork shoulder may be my favorite cut of meat ever and when it's paired with a ton of citrus, salt, and spice, it's unstoppable. I use these carnitas in rice bowls or served with tortillas.

YOU'LL NEED:

FOR THE PORK:
3-4 lb boneless pork shoulder, fat cap trimmed (also called pork butt)
1 tbsp dried oregano
2 tsp salt
2 tsp garlic powder
2 tsp ground cumin
1 tsp onion powder
1 tsp crushed red pepper
½ tsp freshly cracked black pepper

¾ cup fresh orange juice (about 2 oranges)
¼ cup fresh lime juice (about 1 lime)
1 tbsp extra virgin olive oil

FOR FINISHING:
Kosher salt
Fresh lime wedges
Chopped cilantro

1. If cooking immediately, preheat a water bath using an immersion circulator to 165 degrees F.

2. Using a sharp knife, cut pork shoulder into large chunks, about 2 inches wide.

3. Whisk together all remaining ingredients for the pork.

4. Transfer the pork and marinade mixture to a bag of your choice. Massage to coat the pork in the marinade. Remove the air and seal using your method of choice.

5. At this point, you can freeze the pork or cook immediately.

6. Cook in a water bath preheated to 165 degrees F for 12-16 horus (16 hours if frozen).

7. Remove the meat from the bag (keep bag liquid). Shred the meat by inserting two forks and pulling them apart.

8. Heat a cast iron skillet over medium high heat. Add the shredded meat, about ½ cup of the bag liquid, and a generous sprinkle of salt. Cook the meat, flipping occasionally, until crispy and golden brown. Don't crowd the skillet; this may need to be done in batches.

9. Serve in rice bowls or with tortillas with fresh limes and cilantro to garnish.

SPICY SALMON
WITH LEMON DILL BROWN BUTTER

SERVES 4

I came up with this recipe after the recipes for the book were finalized, but it was so delicious I couldn't help but include it. The spicy salmon paired with the rich and lemony brown butter sauce is the ultimate combination. In fact, this is my new favorite way to serve salmon! Serve this with something carby to soak up the butter sauce, such as couscous, the Crispy Potatoes on page 123, mashed potatoes, or simply crusty bread.

YOU'LL NEED:

FOR THE SALMON:
1 pound salmon, skin on or skinless, pin bones removed (can be 1 large piece or multiple pieces)
1 tbsp extra virgin olive oil
Spicy Rub (page 55)

LEMON DILL BROWN BUTTER:
6 tbsp salted butter, cut into 6 pieces
2 tbsp fresh lemon juice (about half a lemon)
2 tbsp chopped fresh dill

1. If cooking immediately, preheat a water bath using an immersion circulator to your desired temperature from page 39.

2. Lightly coat the salmon with the olive oil. Season with the rub so it's completely coated in a thin layer. Place in your bag of choice and remove air and seal using your method of choice.

3. At this point, you can freeze the salmon or cook immediately.

4. When ready to cook, add the salmon to the preheated water bath and cook for 30 minutes or 45 minutes if cooking from frozen.

5. Position an oven rack about 4 inches from the top of your oven. Preheat your oven's broiler to high. Line a rimmed baking sheet with foil.

6. Meanwhile, add the butter to a small saucepan set over medium-low heat. Cook, stirring occasionally, until the butter is completely melted and begins to foam, 5-8 minutes. Once the milk solids on the bottom of the pan begin to turn nutty brown, remove the pan from the heat. Add the lemon juice and dill and stir to combine. Set aside.

7. When the salmon is done sous viding, remove from the bag and place on the foil-lined baking sheet. Discard the bag and its contents. Broil the salmon until the top is just starting to brown, about 2-3 minutes.

8. Spoon the brown butter sauce over the salmon and serve immediately.

SIDES
SIDES
SIDES
SIDES
SIDES

LEMONY ASPARAGUS

SERVES 4

"Why would I sous vide asparagus when I can do it another way?" 1. You can go from freezer to sous vide! 2. As with all other sous vided things, the texture of this asparagus is absolutely perfect. It has a great bite while being tender and the melted butter and lemon make a delicious sauce.

YOU'LL NEED:

1 lb of asparagus, woody ends removed
2 tbsp salted butter, cut into 4 pieces
½ tsp garlic powder
½ tsp kosher salt
¼ tsp freshly cracked black pepper
2 tbsp fresh lemon juice (about ½ lemon)

1. If cooking immediately, preheat a water bath using an immersion circulator to 180 degrees F.

2. Add asparagus, salt, pepper, and garlic powder to a bag of your choice. Shake it to disperse seasoning. Add butter to the bag and spread evenly. Remove the air and seal using your method of choice, doing your best to keep the asparagus in a single layer.

3. At this point you can freeze the asparagus or cook.

4. When ready to cook, add the asparagus to the preheated water bath and cook for 12 minutes, 15 minutes if cooking from frozen.

5. Once done, open the bag and shake around to evenly coat stalks in seasoning and butter. Pour lemon juice over the asparagus and toss again.

6. Serve immediately.

MUSTARD ANCHOVY
GREEN BEANS

SERVES 4

Sous vide green beans are great, but especially so if you're a gardener. Do some minimal prep, freeze, and you've got a ready made side at your disposal! While I recognize "anchovy" may scare some of you off on sight, the umami punch is just what these crisp green beans need.

YOU'LL NEED:

4 anchovy fillets
2 garlic cloves, minced
1 tbsp fresh lemon juice (about ¼ lemon)
1 tbsp Dijon mustard
2 tsp white wine vinegar

1 tsp extra virgin olive oil
1 tsp kosher salt
½ tsp freshly cracked black pepper
1 lb green beans, washed and ends trimmed

1. If cooking immediately, preheat a water bath using an immersion circulator to 186 degrees F.

2. Mix together all ingredients except green beans in a small bowl using a fork. Mash the anchovies into small pieces with the fork.

3. Add the green beans and anchovy mixture to your bag of choice and remove the air using your method of choice, trying to keep the green beans in as flat a layer as possible.

4. At this point, you can freeze the green beans or cook.

5. To cook, place the bag in the preheated water bath and make sure the contents are completely submerged (I like to use a ceramic plate or silicone coated magnets).

6. Cook for 30 minutes for green beans with a snap and 50 minutes for a softer texture (add 5 minutes to either time if cooking from frozen).

7. Remove the green beans from the bag and transfer to a serving plate. Pour the liquid from the bag over the green beans and serve immediately.

GARLIC BUTTER
GREEN BEANS

SERVES 4

Real talk: When I was a kid, I loved nothing more than canned green beans, microwaved and topped with butter and garlic salt. I would happily eat this as a meal. This recipe is a grown-up, much, much better version of my childhood favorite. If only 7 year old Chelsea knew what she was missing.

YOU'LL NEED:

4 tbsp salted butter
1 tbsp fresh lemon juice (about ¼ lemon)
1 tsp garlic powder
½ tsp kosher salt
1 lb green beans, washed and ends trimmed

Grated Parmesan for serving (optional)

1. If cooking immediately, preheat a water bath using immersion circulator to 186 degrees F.

2. Add the butter to a small saucepan over low heat to melt. Once melted, remove from heat. Stir in lemon, garlic powder, and salt.

3. Add the beans and butter mixture to your bag of choice and remove the air using your method of choice, trying to keep the green beans in as flat a layer as possible.

4. At this point, you can freeze the green beans or cook.

5. To cook, place the bag in the preheated water bath and make sure the contents are completely submerged (I like to use a ceramic plate or silicone coated magnets).

6. Cook for 30 minutes for green beans with a snap and 50 minutes for a softer texture (add 5 minutes to either time if cooking from frozen).

7. Remove the green beans from the bag and transfer to a serving plate. Pour the liquid from the bag over the green beans. Top with grated Parmesan if desired.

SPICY LIME
GLAZED CARROTS

SERVES 4 TO 6

I love these carrots - they have a great zing and so much fresh flavor! Although the ingredients make this side seem summery, they're delicious served anytime of the year. I love them next to something hearty, like a ribeye steak.

YOU'LL NEED:

1 lb carrots, trimmed, peeled, and halved lengthwise and crosswise
1 jalapeno, ribs and seeds removed, finely chopped
2 tbsp fresh lime juice (about 1 lime)
1 tbsp honey

1 tbsp extra olive oil
½ tsp kosher salt
½ tsp garlic powder
¼ tsp freshly cracked black pepper
¼ tsp ground cumin

¼ cup chopped cilantro, for serving

1. If cooking immediately, preheat a water bath using immersion circulator to 185 degrees F.

2. Add all ingredients except cilantro to a bag of your choice and toss to combine a bit, evenly dispersing the butter. Remove the air and seal using your method of choice, keeping the carrots in as flat a layer as possible.

3. At this point, you can freeze the carrots or cook.

4. To cook, place bag in preheated water bath and make sure the contents are completely submerged (I like to use a ceramic plate or silicone coated magnets). Cook for 1 hour (add 10 minutes if cooking from frozen).

5. When done sous viding, add just the carrots to a large skillet over medium-high heat (keep the liquid in the bag!). Saute until carrots have just begun to brown and caramelize, about 3-4 minutes on each side.

6. Add the liquid from the bag to the skillet and cook until reduced, about 3 minutes.

7. Transfer the carrots to a serving bowl and spoon the sauce over top. Serve immediately.

HONEY THYME
GLAZED CARROTS

SERVES 4 TO 6

These carrots are excellent served on the side of almost any main dish. Fresh thyme, honey, and butter make for a delicate but balanced flavor. You might be thinking, "I can cook carrots a dozen other ways, is an hour in the water bath really worth it?" I promise, once you try this method, you'll see the magic and never want to cook carrots another way again!

YOU'LL NEED:

1 lb carrots, trimmed, peeled, and halved lengthwise and crosswise
4 tbsp salted butter, sliced into 4 pats
2 tbsp honey
½ tsp chopped fresh thyme leaves
½ tsp kosher salt
¼ tsp freshly cracked black pepper

1. If cooking immediately, preheat a water bath using immersion circulator to 185 degrees F.

2. Add all ingredients to a bag of your choice and toss to combine a bit, evenly dispersing the butter. Remove the air and seal using your method of choice, keeping the carrots in as flat a layer as possible.

3. At this point, you can freeze the carrots or cook.

4. To cook, place bag in preheated water bath and make sure the contents are completely submerged (I like to use a ceramic plate or silicone coated magnets). Cook for 1 hour (add 10 minutes if cooking from frozen).

5. When done sous viding, add just the carrots to a large skillet over medium-high heat (keep the liquid in the bag!). Saute until carrots have just begun to brown and caramelize, about 3-4 minutes on each side.

6. Add the liquid from the bag to the skillet and cook until reduced, about 3 minutes.

7. Transfer the carrots to a serving bowl and spoon the sauce over top. Serve immediately.

GARLIC BUTTER
CORN ON THE COB

SERVES 4

Who doesn't love buttery corn on the cob? With this method, you can stock your freezer with corn while it's in season, then pull it out and put it right in the water bath when you're ready to eat it. Yes, it takes a bit to cook, but with sous vide it will be cooked absolutely perfectly every time.

YOU'LL NEED:

4 ears of corn, shucked
½ cup salted butter, cut into 8 pats
1 tsp kosher salt
1 tsp garlic powder

2 tbsp chopped parsley, for serving

1. If cooking immediately, preheat a water bath using an immersion circulator to 181 degrees F.

2. Add all ingredients except parsley to a bag of your choice and toss to combine a bit, evenly dispersing the butter. Remove the air and seal using your method of choice, keeping the ears of corn in a flat layer.

3. At this point, you can freeze the corn or cook immediately.

4. To cook, place the bag of corn in the preheated water bath and make sure the contents are completely submerged (I like to use a ceramic plate or silicone coated magnets). Cook for 30 minutes (40 minutes if cooking from frozen).

5. Place on a serving plate and pour the liquid from the bag over the corn. Sprinkle with parsley and serve immediately.

PARMESAN POLENTA

SERVES 4

I love polenta. Creamy, smooth, and if I have my way, cheesy thanks to plenty of parmesan. I don't make it often because I find whatever pot I make it in is near impossible to clean afterwards. Enter sous vide! It's nearly as simple as dumping all your ingredients in a bag and letting the immersion circulator do its thing. And yes, this recipe is freezer-friendly!

YOU'LL NEED:

1 cup polenta (also called coarse cornmeal)
2 cups chicken or vegetable stock
2 cups milk (1%, 2% or whole)
2 tbsp salted butter, melted

1 tsp salt
½ tsp black pepper
½ cup grated Parmesan

1. If cooking immediately, preheat a water bath using an immersion circulator to 185 degrees F.

2. Add all ingredients except Parmesan to a bag of your choice. Remove the air from the bag using your method of choice and seal. Shake bag to combine the ingredients.

3. At this point you can freeze the polenta or cook immediately.

4. When ready to cook, cook for 2 hours in the preheated water bath.

5. When finished, pour the contents of the bag into a serving bowl. Stir in the grated Parmesan. Taste and adjust salt and pepper to your liking.

HERBY RISOTTO

SERVES 4

Let's be real: Risotto is a pain in the butt to make. It requires so much babysitting. And yes, the payoff is wonderful, but at what cost?! With sous vide risotto, you just add all the ingredients to a bag and cook it! No hovering and adding liquid and tasting and adding more liquid over and over and over. You're going to love this risotto that's packed with herby flavor and plenty of cheesy goodness.

YOU'LL NEED:

1 cup arborio rice
2 ¼ cups chicken or vegetable broth
2 tbsp fresh lemon juice (about ½ lemon)
1 tbsp olive oil
2 tsp Italian seasoning

1 tsp garlic powder
1 tsp kosher salt
½ tsp freshly cracked black pepper
½ cup grated Parmesan

1. If cooking immediately, preheat water bath using immersion circulator to 185 degrees F.

2. Add all ingredients except Parmesan to a bag of your choice. Remove the air from the bag using your method of choice and seal. Shake bag to combine the ingredients.

3. At this point you can freeze the risotto or cook immediately.

4. When ready to cook, cook for 45 minutes in the preheated water bath, 55 minutes if cooking from frozen.

5. When finished, pour the contents of the bag into a serving bowl. Stir in the grated Parmesan. Taste and adjust salt and pepper to your liking.

Index

ACKNOWLEDGMENTS

First of all, thank you to my amazing husband, Eric, who blindly encourages and supports every wild idea I come up with (there's a lot of 'em) and simlutaneously keeps me sane by making sure I set aside plenty of time for camping, beach trips, movie nights, and bar hops, even when it takes a lot of effort to pull myself away from said projects. Thank you for trying every single recipe in this book, even if I wasn't always satisfied with your feedback ("It's really good!" "But what do you think of xyz?" "It's great!"). I love you.

Thank you to my mom and dad, who I know had a couple of panic attacks when my career started to veer towards the unconventional but love it now and remind me constantly just how proud they are of me and do everything they can to support me. Thank you, mom, for all the times you've come over to prep food and wash dishes on shoot days and for inspiring this book with your meal prepping ways. Oh, and thank you both for being excellent recipe testers and tasters. I love you.

Thank you to my sweet brother, even though he continuously claimed I never brought enough food for him to try. I'm so lucky to have you. I love you.

Thank you to my sister-in-law, Amy, who contributed so much to this project and never failed to give me pep talks.

Thank you to Mara, my amazing virtual assistant, for knowing how I work so well and making every part of my business a thousand times easier.

Thank you to my fellow food bloggers and friends, many of whom I've never even met, for being some of my biggest cheerleaders through this process. Including Ashley, who let me include one of her recipes in this book and Sarah, who edited and indexed this book.

Thank you to Jason Logsdon, Mike LaCharite, and the International Sous Vide Association community for the support and enthusiasm.

Thank you to my mentor, Diane Morgan, for recipe testing, recipe editing, and teaching me so much.

Thank you to Carly Jayne, my incredibly creative friend, idea partner, and 911 graphic designer and Adobe wiz.

Thank you to all of my wonderful recipes testers, who include family, friends, internet friends, and total strangers:

Laurie Miller (hi, mom!)
Debbie Cole (hi, MIL!)
Amy Pedersen
Tami Grabinski
Michelle Tech
Karen McLeese
Carly Courie
Bob Cotter
Richard Jensen
Marisa Kerkvliet
Sarah Nenninger
Kate Moritz
Heahter Bilyeu
Jessica Kisky
Diane Morgan
Graham Jones
Heather Fogg
Beverly Palmer
Ashley Walker